AFTER
LAW
SCHOOL?

CARTER, LEDYARD & MILBURN
COUNSELLORS AT LAW
54 WALL STREET
NEW YORK

LEWIS CASS LEDYARD
JOHN S. MILBURN
EDMUND L. BAYLIES
GEORGE A. MILLER
LEWIS CASS LEDYARD, JR.

WALTER F. TAYLOR
JOSEPH W. WELSH

June 10th, 1907.

Mr. F. Roosevelt,
135 East 36th Street,
New York City.

Dear Mr. Roosevelt:-

    I have talked over with Mr. Ledard the question of your coming to our office, and I find that we can arrange to have a place for you at such time as you may wish to come here in the autumn, not later than October 1st, preferably a week or so earlier.

    In case you come to us the arrangement with you will be the same as we usually make in such cases, that is to say, you will come to us the first year without salary, and after you have been with us for a year we would expect, if you remain, to pay you a salary which, however, at the outset would necessarily be rather small.

    Very truly yours,

Edmund L. Baylies

Edmund L. Baylies*

---

*Facsimile of an actual letter sent to an aspiring law school graduate

AFTER
LAW
SCHOOL?

Finding a Job
in a Tight Market

Saul Miller

Little, Brown and Company
Boston   Toronto

"When one said that the number of lawyers would mar the occupation, he answered, 'No, for always the more spaniels in the field, the more the game.'"

—*Proverb*

Contents

Preface

"The lawyer is, I claim, the highest product of human evolution. The civilization of any nation may be measured by the number of its lawyers. It is not necessary for me to prove in this place and before this audience that the United States is the most civilized nation in the world, and the statistics show that it has twice as many lawyers in proportion to its population as any other country has. England comes next in the degree of its civilization and in the number of its lawyers. France and Germany follow. Russia has more priests and less lawyers in proportion to the population than any other country in Europe, and if you pass over to the Orient, where modern civilization is struggling with ancient barbarism, you have to search far and long before you can find a lawyer of any kind."

Walter S. Logan in an address
before the Women Lawyers' Club
of New York City — 1905

"San Francisco Feminist 35, professional, together, athletic, joyous, seeks male 25 to 40 with whom to share prurient and other interests. Please be tall, passionately intellectual, divorced, and not a lawyer. NYR, Box 9072."

A personal ad appearing in The
New York Review of Books — 1973

This is a book about looking for a law job in what is now a very tight job market. Although it will be of greatest interest to law students looking for part-time, summer and full-time positions, it will also be of great use to practicing attorneys who want to change jobs. It should be especially interesting to those attorneys who have been out of law school for up to about five years.

In addition, undergraduates or anyone else who is contemplating going to law school will find the book helpful. After all, job prospects for law graduates are of prime concern to those interested in applying to law school. Also, since the book delineates literally hundreds of different jobs available to law graduates, it is a long overdue antidote to the limited, stereotypic portrait of opportunities displayed by the mass media. For this reason, the book will be a valuable counseling guide for undergraduate school law career advisers. And, of course, law school placement officers will find it to be an essential resource.

Looking for law positions is in many respects no different than job hunting in other fields. However, law placement apparently does have certain unique (and seemingly unfortunate) characteristics. For example, in no other field is on-campus recruitment so visible. In no other field do students expect to secure their job several months or even a year before they are prepared to start work. And in no other field has the placement office come to assume such an important role.

These characteristics are unfortunate because they have come to be thought of as the norm, when, in fact, they are merely "apparent," i.e. they describe relatively few law schools and portray the experiences of but a handful of law students and law graduates. About 700 recruiters interview at Harvard Law School each year and account for about 90% of the job offers Harvard students receive. About 500 employers recruit at

Yale, and interviewers in the hundreds also recruit on-campus at other "upper echelon" law schools. These same schools send newsletters to their graduates with listings of jobs from around the country. However, the overwhelming majority of law schools have small or no on-campus recruitment programs and offer few job listings to their alumnae(i). This is the real norm, and the one to which the book speaks.

Although the book addresses itself primarily to the needs of those people who look for jobs on their own, it is hoped that students and graduates of the so-called favored schools will also read it. Perhaps they will come to resist the temptation of so readily entrusting their fates to their schools' recruitment programs. When I visited Harvard Law School, a major complaint voiced by students was the pressure they felt to accept jobs with the corporate firms that recruit there each fall. Because those pay more and recruit more visibly and earlier than other employers, the temptation to accept their offers was almost irresistible. Or, in the words of the Harvard Law School Placement Director: "It's not seduction, it's rape!"

WHAT THIS BOOK IS NOT

A Guaranteed Method for Getting You a Job. There is no scientific approach to job hunting, which if pursued step by step will give you a predictable result. Therefore, this book cannot claim to offer such a programmed course of action. In fact, great pains will be taken to show the deleterious consequences of thinking of job hunting as a science, as a particular system with prescribed *do*s and *don't*s. Rather than a monolithic approach to finding a job, to be pursued by all people for all positions, this book talks about many different approaches. This is necessary since different people, with their own temperament, needs and career interests, should look for a job in their own way and in their own style.

Rather than guaranteed results, this book talks about creating a momentum out of which a satisfying result is likely to come, although not in any kind of precise or predictable way. In fact, it is this unpredictability that can make job hunting interesting, exciting and even fun.

A Guide to the Best Places to Work. The book does not make judgments about the merits of working in one job over another. It doesn't attempt to identify the "best" positions for students or graduates. It does not talk about work settings in terms of mobility within and without. And it doesn't discuss the relative merits of such things as specialization.

Nor does the book discuss what it is like to work in different settings. What it's like to work for a small firm compared to a large one. What a big city practice is like compared to a suburban practice. The work of a prosecutor compared to that of a public defender. Private practice as opposed to government work. Or, private practice as opposed to working in the legal department of a corporation.

Instead, the book focuses on the job search itself. However, in discussing materials and people to be used in that search, it will put you in touch with the very same resources that will be able to speak to those issues and make those value judgments that it does not.

WHAT THIS BOOK IS
A Discussion of Ideas, Strategies and Tactics for Job Hunting. The book will help you find out the kinds of opportunities that are available. It will help you identify specific openings and will suggest strategies to be used in applying for them.

Much of the information can be used in a generalized way since it applies to various kinds of positions. Other information is more specific and is only appropriate in relation to looking for particular types of jobs. However, all approaches share the trait that they are intended to lead you to more and more people and places, and from out of that network — out of that momentum — will come opportunities and, ultimately, job offers.

A Compilation of Printed Resource Materials. There is an infinite amount of printed material available that can be used in job hunting. The book catalogues these resources. They include some of the more obvious ones such as *Martindale-Hubbell,* as well as the less obvious, though no less valuable, resources. In fact, the latter group can often be much more valuable since fewer applicants for jobs will be using them. Very few people interested in applying for a job with a private firm don't at some point resort to *Martindale* for a list of firms to which to write. As a result, very many people wind up applying to the exact same places. However, few people would think to write to someone mentioned in a newspaper article as the attorney for a union, a particular criminal defendant, an environmental group, a firm or some other client.

The book lists directories, journals, newsletters, newspapers, books, telephone directories, annual reports, bar association publications and other published materials. It details ways of obtaining these materials. Most are readily obtainable, and if it is not feasible for an individual to get them, they can usually be found in a law school placement office (which should get them if they haven't already), a law library or a public library.

An Explanation of How to Use Resource Materials. Knowing that a particular resource exists and knowing how to use it are two different things. Even such a common directory as *Martindale-Hubbell* is typically used unimaginatively and inexhaustively. People rarely look at anything but the biographical section of *Martindale.* There is, in fact, a front section which is a much more comprehensive listing of attorneys and firms. Also, few people know that a Volume VI exists, and that it contains lots of useful information including a state-by-state listing of "Public Interest Practice Firms and Organizations."

The book tries to give you ideas about utilizing the resources that are not so obvious. The only limits on the resources available to you are your own knowledge of them and your imagination. It is hoped that this book will sensitize you to where and how to get information. As a Director of Placement, I often discovered new places by reading *The New York Times* nuptial announcements!

A Discussion of How to Find People Who Can Help You. Law students and graduates tend to be very impatient when it comes to finding a job. One manifestation of this impatience is to expect a job offer (or at least the discovery of a job opening) to result from every letter written, every phone call made, any placement symposium attended, and any encounter with a practicing attorney. One of the unfortunate aspects of this attitude, aside from the obvious frustrations and disappointments that occur, is that it prevents you from thinking about using opportunities and people merely for the purpose of obtaining additional information that could be helpful in your job search. If you wrote to a labor lawyer only to inquire about a position in that attorney's firm, s/he would be reluctant to meet with you if no opening was available. However, that same attorney might be very willing to see you if you made it clear that what you really wanted to find out was the name of lawyers, firms and organizations in that geographic area that you could contact about a position in labor law. You must learn to give people the opportunity to respond positively to you. To ask for a job where no opening exists, is not such an opportunity. To ask for information at that same place, could be.

This book, then, discusses specific ways of finding and using people from whom to obtain more information. It talks about attending conferences, conventions and continuing legal education programs to meet lawyers practicing in a particular field. It discusses, for example, the potential wealth of information students and graduates have for each other if they would not be so protective of that information in terms of the "competition."

One of the most frustrating aspects of looking for a job is the feeling that you have exhausted all possibilities. Someone sends out resumes to 100 firms, gets no interviews and can't think of another possible place to write. It is the intent of this book to give you ideas for avoiding such impasses or, at least, getting over them.

Acknowledgments

I would like to thank the many legal employers who allowed me to interview them. Thanks also go to the many law school placement offices that provided me with information. The placement offices at New York University, University of Connecticut, Suffolk University, Harvard University and George Washington University law schools were particularly generous with their time and information.

Very special thanks go to Alice Miller for her manuscript suggestions and more, Helen Wensley of Hofstra Law School for typing the manuscript, Molly Geraghty of Northeastern Law School for introducing me to "Ephraim Tutt," and to Hank Haverstick and Lori Mogol of Brooklyn Law School for accommodating my every request.

How It 1
Used To Be

"In John Adams' diary, it is said, there were but eight persons actively engaged in the practice of law in Boston in 1763, and Adams himself was the only one of these practicing in Boston after the revolution."

John L. Cadwalader
in a lecture on the Conduct
of the Legal Life —1894

This chapter is devoted to excerpts from *Yankee Lawyer — The Autobiography of Ephraim Tutt*. It traces Tutt's law placement history starting with how he obtained his first job after graduating third in his class from the Harvard Law School in 1894. The opportunities that came to Tutt, including an offer of a judgeship on the United States Circuit Court of Appeals, which he refused, were partly due to his own making and partly due to luck. However, he was prepared to be lucky, and by his receptiveness and his sense of adventure, he increased his chances to be lucky.

Times have certainly changed since Ephraim Tutt began his legal career. Circumstances for the law graduate today are much different. There are now about 450,000 lawyers in the United States. Almost 40,000 practicing in New York City alone! About 125,000 law students are enrolled in accredited law schools around the country, and more than 30,000 new attorneys are admitted to the bar each year. Aside from the vast number of lawyers entering the job market, thus creating great pressure on the market to absorb them, other circumstances have changed since Tutt's time that have contributed to reducing peoples' sense of adventure — their sense of "striking off" into a career. Law students today often graduate with several thousand dollars of education loan debts. Many law graduates today are older than the typical graduate of the past, and often have family financial obligations that dictate certain constraints on what they can do with their law degree. Also, many law students now begin law school after pursuing another career for several years and therefore are patient with a slowly evolving legal career.

However, the changes are more extensive than these. There have been some other fundamental changes that have come to make today's law graduate face the job market with dread, timidity, and a pervasive conservatism. Not the least of these changes has been the institutionalization of law placement through placement offices, on-campus recruiting, summer internship programs, and the establishment of a hierarchy of what are the so-called choice positions. Therefore, I hope that these excerpts can be instructive for recapturing a spirit that existed when placement offices and the like did not. And, even if this account from times gone by is not instructive, it is rather delightful.

By virtue of graduating third in his class and being a member of *The Harvard Law Review*, Tutt was invited to interview with the prestigious Boston firm of Curtis, Jones & Mason.

. . . [R]eporting at the office of Curtis, Jones & Mason [1] was ushered into the august presence of the senior partner, at the moment engaged in having his shoes polished while smoking a cigar. Mr. Curtis, who was pink and obviously well fed, wore a carefully parted "ferry-slip" and, in spite of the odor of legal sanctity surrounding him, I had an unreasonable desire to kick him in the pants.

"We-ell?" he remarked coldly as if I had intruded upon some intimate personal function.

"My name is Ephraim Tutt," I explained. "I have a letter from your firm asking me to call."

"H'm!" he muttered scrutinizing me. "Oh, yes. I remember, Professor Gray recommended you, I believe. Well, you look as if you had some sense. What are your politics?"

"I voted for President Cleveland."

He grunted.

"A 'mug-wump,' I suppose? Well, we'll overlook that if you haven't any other crazy ideas. You may report to our chief clerk."

"How much shall I be paid?" I ventured.

"What! — Do you expect to be paid" he demanded as if outraged. "Most young men are glad to come into my firm for the experience. However, if you need it, I'll give you five dollars a week. — By the way," he added, running his eye over my costume, "I suggest that you wear a stand-up collar instead of the thing you have on. — That will be all for the moment."

His smugness infuriated me.

"I'll change my collar if you'll change your beard!" I retorted.

"Well, I'll be — ," he exploded.

"Damned," I finished for him.

Tutt didn't get the job. However, he did get a very good job lead from his friend Angus McGillicuddy, who apparently kept an eye on the obituary columns for promising opportunities.

"I know just the place for you," he assured me. "Pottsville, New York, in the Mohawk Valley, a pleasant little town with several fine trout streams in the neighborhood. The only good lawyer in the place — Judge Eben Wynkoop — died a couple of years ago. You might take over his practice. Come along!"

So they took off (on bicycles!) from Cambridge for Pottsville.

. . . Angus, having shown me his favorite pools on Chasm Brook, pedalled off to the Adirondacks, while I settled myself comfortably in a corner room at Ma Best's overlooking the square, for which, with meals included, she charged me $7 per week. Ma ran the hotel herself without assistance save for her daughter Betty, a smart girl of fifteen, Willie Toothaker, a toothless, freckled, redheaded urchin who was something of a mechanical genius, and Joe, a Negro boy who looked after the horses, handled the luggage and, since there was no electricity in the town, cleaned the kerosene lamps. Between them they did all the work and did it very well, except during such periods as the hotel was over-crowded owing to the circus or a trial term of the Supreme Court. . . .

At that time there was only one lawyer in the town, Hezekiah Mason, a thick-set, ruddy faced man of about my own age, with a spade beard, a square derby hat, and a curt manner.

"He's got all the law business now, such as it is," Ma explained to me. "He's smart all right, but personally I wouldn't trust him around the corner. It was a pity old Judge Wynkoop had to die. He was a great man and the biggest lawyer this side of Albany. No one would ha' thought of goin' to Mason while the Judge was alive, even if he was eighty-two. His office was right across the street from here — that sort of little temple with green shutters and pillars? I've got the key. Want to take a look at it?"

The dust rose in clouds, and a dead squirrel dropped off the window sill, as I pushed open the shutters and let the daylight stream into Judge Wynkoop's former demesne. . . . Books lined the walls to the ceiling on three sides, a Franklin stove stood in a corner and a black walnut desk between the windows. In the rear was a coal bin and small coat closet. Save that all his private papers had been removed the place doubtless was exactly as the Judge had left it.

I rented the Greek Temple for $5 per month, books and all, and nailed up my first sign — black letters on a white ground — on the horse-chestnut tree in front — "Ephraim Tutt — Attorney and Counsellor-at-law." All I needed was clients.

The lack of clients was not his only problem.

I was a mature and presumably well-educated young man, who for three years had studied such profound and esoteric doctrines as *"cy pres"* and *"equitable conversion,"* yet not since my boyhood had I heard a case tried in court. I did not know how to frame a complaint or answer, to draw a will or a lease, or even how to fill out a summons or subpoena. I was like some young lady who, having taken cooking lessons, could prepare *"cotellette d'Agneau a la Soubraise"* but was unable to fry an egg. . . .

My shingle swayed in the breeze for several weeks without flagging any clients, and I had plenty of time to explore the possibilities of the neighboring brooks. My new fellow townsmen were friendly but showed no disposition to beat a path to the door of my office, and I began to wonder what made them so shy of me. Did I, perhaps, look too young to be a lawyer? Then one day while poking about in Judge Wynkoop's closet I stumbled upon an old stovepipe hat and ivory-headed cane which must have been his. The hat was shabby and cracked, and the silk was so ruffed and worn that in spots it was almost bare, but it fitted me exactly. "Well," thought I, "it won't cost me anything to wear it and see what happens."

That evening I paraded around the square and, strangely enough, the very next morning acquired a client. . . .

After four years of practice in Pottsville, Tutt decided to leave and continue to pursue his law career in New York City. However, in fairness to those who sing the praises of small town practice, Tutt left Pottsville less out of a disenchantment with country lawyering than as the result of an unfortunate romance with a married woman who continued to live in Pottsville.

I had brought with me a few letters of introduction from Judge Tompkins and a certificate from the Pottsville branch of the Sacred Camels of King Menelik to the local lodge of the brotherhood in New York to the effect that I was a member in good standing, but the Judge's friends proved to be in an advanced state of legal decay and my brother Camels while friendly, unable to advance my professional interests. I assiduously followed up the advertisements for legal help in the Law Journal and visited such lawyers as were suggested by Otto without result. No one, however, seemed impressed by my qualifications and having tramped from one office to another for several weeks without finding an opening, I began to wonder whether, without friends or connections, I should ever be able to get a foothold.

One evening I was taking a turn on Fifth Avenue when a thickset man with a scraggy beard, who was about to cross Fiftieth Street in front of me, slipped on the curb and fell heavily to the sidewalk. I helped him to his feet, held him upright while he tested his legs, and then retrieved his tall hat from the gutter.

"I'm afraid I've sprained my ankle!" he said wincing.

"Shall I call a cab?" I asked.

"No," he said. "Give me your arm and I'll go back to the Club."

Well, "the Club" turned out to be Tammany Hall, and the thickset fellow with the scraggy beard turned out to be Boss Croker. And, as a result of this chance encounter Tutt was offered a position as an assistant district attorney with the Manhattan District Attorney's Office. Tutt was very successful as a prosecutor, and after three years was offered the position of First Trial Assistant. However, he had always been somewhat disturbed with the role of a prosecutor, preferring instead to be on the defense side. So, he turned down the offer and with Bonnie Doon, one of the investigators in the DA's office, he struck out on his own.

I rented a small office on Franklin Street within a stone's throw of the Criminal Courts Building, hung out my shingle again and waited for clients. At first I was sadly disappointed by the result. I had assumed from occasionally having seen my name in print and having been treated with exaggerated deference by the hangers on of the criminal courts, that I was a person of distinction if not already famous, but I soon found that an ex-deputy-assistant-district attorney was a dead dog so far as the general public was concerned. I was just another chap out of a job, and competing for a living with the rest of the criminal bar. My income dropped from several hundred dollars a month to practically nothing. . . .

Yet now as I look back, I can see that this interim was one of the pleasanter periods of my life. I was absolutely my own master, beholden to no one for a salary. I needed to earn but ten dollars a week to live, and another ten for my office rent, since Bonnie had agreed to work for nothing provided he received half of the fees he might bring in, and before long he brought in plenty of them. I won't say it was the highest class of law practice, but it paid and sometimes paid well, for Bonnie, as a process server, had a wide acquaintance with the foreign born. He was a natural salesman with a ready tongue, and he lost no opportunity to advertise the fact that one of the greatest and most eloquent lawyers of all time was for the moment at liberty to accept retainers — provided they came quick enough.

Tutt had been in private practice on his own for about a year when he was offered an opportunity to join a major Wall Street firm as a junior partner at a salary of $5,000 a year (it is now 1902). Against his better judgment, he accepted.

Hotchkiss, Levy & Hogan was a typical Wall Street law factory, occupying two entire stories in a white-stone office building within spitting distance of J. P. Morgan & Co. There were fifteen full-fledged partners who shared a percentage in the profits and, in addition to twenty-eight juniors receiving regular salaries, there were thirty-five law clerks, forty stenographers, four cashiers, eight expert accountants, twelve office boys, a double-shift of telephone operators, a posse of process servers and detectives, a translator, a photographer, a real estate expert, an architectural draftsman and two librarians. The plant was divided into a corporations department, a probate department, a patent department, a personal injuries and trial department, a divorce department, an international law department, and various others, while its total overhead was not far from half a million a year. Its filing system equalled that of Sears Roebuck, the lights burned all night long and luncheon was eaten off trays by all including salaried partners, who came early, stayed late, and died young. . . .

After he had been with Hotchkiss, Levy & Hogan for about five years, Tutt received a letter from his long-time friend Otto Wiegand asking Tutt if he wanted to form a partnership with him. The firm of Wiegand & Tutt was formed and lasted for over 15 years (1907-1923). The firm had an excellent reputation in the New York legal community, and both Otto Wiegand and Ephraim Tutt pursued illustrious careers. Wiegand was offered a judgeship on the New York Supreme Court and Tutt was offered a judgeship on the United States Circuit Court of Appeals by Calvin Coolidge (at the suggestion of Oliver Wendell Holmes, whom Tutt knew very well). Although Tutt turned down his offer, Otto Wiegand did accept a position on the New York court, so at the age of 54 Tutt was a single practitioner again. But not for long. Very soon after, Tutt was to form the final partnership of his legal career. It happened one day when Ephraim Tutt's secretary announced that there was a Mr. Tutt to see him.

"Tutt?" I exclaimed. "I thought I was the one and only Tutt — anyhow in this neck of the woods! Show him in by all means!"

The new Tutt was a stocky, bespectacled, carefully dressed man between forty-five and fifty, with a pronounced abdominal convexity, round red cheeks, and a pointed nose. . .

"My name's Tutt, Mr. Tutt," he said. "Samuel. Any opening in your office?"

He looked in fact exactly as a man named Tutt should look.

"I don't know," I answered. "Why do you come to me?"

"Because with you I should be associated with a good name," he answered seriously, although I should have sworn that he winked.

"That might go double," I said. "Where do you come from?"

"Bangor, Maine," he answered. "Belong to the Abijah Tutt branch. You're one of the Elijahs. Same family, though. Twin brothers back in 1635. We're sixteenth cousins. — Not near enough to kiss."

"God forbid!" I said.

"Metaphorically only! My other assets: A.B. and LL.B. University of Maine, five years' practice in Bangor, ten years in New York as managing clerk for Nickerson, Spratt and Greely — five years by myself. — Don't get on with my wife. — Like work. Keeps me away from her." . . . At that moment Chief Justice II [Tutt's dog] emerged from under the table, sniffed Tutt critically around the pant-cuffs, then placing his paws on one of the carefully creased trouser-legs wagged his tail. "Woof!" he said, meaning "Judgment for the plaintiff."

"You have been approved by the Committee on Admissions," I said. "It so happens that I've just been called away on important business. I shall be gone about three weeks. You can take over in my absence and, if the office is still here on my return and no one has sued me for malpractice, we can talk turkey."

And that was the origin of the very successful partnership of Tutt & Tutt.

Ephraim Tutt probably never wrote a resume!

Resumes 2

"Only if the person is from a top law school will I read the entire resume."

*A hiring partner
with a New York City firm which,
during the fall,
receives 30 resumes a day*

"I pay no attention to resumes. Since you can't tell anything from them, I'll grant an interview to anyone who requests one."

*An interviewer for
a criminal defenders program*

There is no consensus as to what comprises a good resume in terms of length, content or style. Every employer who considers resumes has different notions and expectations about them. Some employers would not look at a resume that was more than one page. Most couldn't care less. Many employers like — and even request — a photograph on the resume. Many others are actually offended by its inclusion. A professionally printed and reproduced resume impresses some people. Others question the judgment and values of an applicant who would make such an effort and incur the expense.

Although this chapter ends with sample resumes, you will do yourself a disservice if you adopt the samples as models for preparing your own resume. The samples are included primarily to illustrate points rather than as absolute models of what is a good resume. Also, your resume should be expressive of *your* personality, not someone else's whose resume style you have copied.

SOME GENERAL COMMENTS	A major problem relating to resumes is the undue importance that job applicants often place on them. A resume is not an essential ingredient in every job-hunting scenario. In fact, a resume should only be necessary when other more preferable and more natural ways of getting a job fail, e.g., being recommended by a law professor who is intimately aware of your interests and abilities; being offered a job by someone who knows the high quality of your work as a result of an article on which the two of you collaborated; or being offered a full-time position by an employer for whom you have previously worked part-time or during the summer, on a volunteer basis or for pay. A resume, then, is really needed only when a stranger is applying to another stranger for a job, a situation that can often be avoided.

Many of the anxieties and mistakes that go along with preparing a resume grow out of this problem of misplaced importance. Many law graduates and students cling to the notion that there is an ideal resume, and all they have to do is get theirs just right and it will assure them a job. Aside from the fact that there is no such ideal, a resume, at best, can only get you an interview. The quotes at the beginning of the chapter portray some very commonly held attitudes of employers regarding resumes. At one extreme is the person who doesn't look past the law school you attend or from which you graduated. At the other extreme is the employer who will interview anyone regardless of their resume. In most instances a resume is used as a convenience. It is an accepted way of making initial contact, but in the context of those hirers who receive hundreds of applications for a single position, perhaps it is necessary.

This is not to say resumes are unimportant. It is only to say they are not *as* important as many people view them. Thought and care should go into their preparation. There *will* be prospective employers who will not be getting your resume in a batch with 100 others. Therefore, they will be able to read it more carefully and glean more information and draw more conclusions from it than someone inundated with applications. Between the extremes represented by the quotes, there are many hirers who do expect to get a considerable amount of information from the resume, and these are the people you should have in mind when preparing your resume.

Resumes are more often criticized for saying too much rather than too little. Again, this results from a lack of a proper perspective regarding the limitations of resumes. A deputy general counsel for a federal agency related the example of a resume she once received that mentioned the fact that the applicant had been married in a French chateau! Or another that indicated under "Personal Data" that the applicant had no financial debts. And out of this same lack of perspective come the resumes printed on blue, yellow or pink paper.

This problem of attempting to say too much is a predictable outgrowth of the more general problem of looking for a job in a tight market — a job market very often thought to be even tighter than it actually is. From this belief about the job market comes the sense of vulnerability that induces students and graduates to apply for all kinds of jobs as a way of keeping their options open — jobs they are both interested in and qualified for as well as positions for which they have neither an interest nor the credentials. To play this numbers game, applicants make up resumes that attempt to be all things to all employers for all positions.

A common failing of these all-purpose resumes is that they are often unfocused and vague. They don't give a very straightforward and clear portrait of your interests, background or personality. This makes it much more difficult for someone reading your resume — someone with very clearly defined hiring needs — to respond positively to your resume. So, what was done as a way of keeping options open, ironically limits your options.

It is important for applicants to decide, within a reasonable range, what kind of positions they are interested in and qualified for. The question really is, "Whom do you want your resume to impress?" Large corporate law firms, for example, are more exclusively interested in academic credentials than most other employers. Small, suburban law firms are probably more interested in personality traits. A public interest law center will look for prior exposure and experience with issues in the area of its concern. Criminal defenders' and prosecutors' offices will look for trial practice experience as well as some work in criminal law. Poverty law programs will expect applicants to have had some clinical experience. Government agencies often want applicants to demonstrate their interest through courses they have taken relating to the work of that agency.

So, in deciding for whom you are preparing your resume, you will be giving it focus and will be in a better position to decide which information is appropriate —

the same information that would be inappropriate if your resume were to be sent to different employers. The result of this is a resume that you will likely get more mileage from, since employers will more easily be able to connect their hiring needs with you. Sometimes there is even a benefit to be derived from the decision of an employer that you're an inappropriate candidate for a position with them because of your interests and background as you've clearly represented them in your resume. One person who reviews resumes for a federal agency commented that she often gave applications sent to her to people she knew in other agencies when such resumes indicated interests and qualifications more appropriate to that agency and that agency then had positions to fill while hers did not.

Finally, the resume is an excellent way by which you can exert control over an interview. Typically, interviewers will have the resume on their desk or lap during the interview, and will look at it for suggestions of items or topics to discuss. Therefore, by including certain things, or by highlighting some items while understating others, you can usually focus an interviewer's attention on those things in the resume that you want discussed — things which, if talked about in depth, will portray you in a positive way. For example, you might want to encourage discussion of research you have done, an article you have published or a major honor you have earned.

In preparing your resume it's helpful to ask certain questions as a way of deciding what you want to include in the resume and what style to choose. The questions of "Whom do you want to appeal to?" and "What do you want discussed at the interview?" have already been mentioned. In addition, it's helpful to ask, "If I were an

PREPARING THE RESUME

employer, what information would be useful to me in deciding whom I wanted to interview?" Is the fact that someone was born in Santa Barbara, California a helpful bit of additional information in your deciding whether or not to interview that person?

Another question you might want to keep in mind is, "Does this information particularly distinguish me from anyone else?" One interviewer observed that the interests of most educated people are pretty much the same. So, to list your interests as reading, or chess, or travel or community involvement doen't really portray you as any more or less anything than most other people with law degrees. Unless your interests and personal experience are really different, listing them is just puffery.

As to the style of your resume, ask yourself "What will be the context in which the resume will be seen?" If you anticipate that your resume will be sent to employers by your law school along with the resumes of 60 other students, a three-page resume might not get looked at. Although the substance of a resume ultimately is always more important than the form, the form can often obscure, or even hide, crucial items of information. Will the style of the resume — its length, the spacing, indentations, underlinings, capitalizations — enable an employer to quickly see the important things, especially if the resume is on the desk and s/he is periodically glancing down at it during an interview?

Finally, as to both form and content, avoid the easy psychological cliches that get bandied about regarding resumes. Many people will 'list the ten college, law school and community offices to which they've been elected on the assumption this will show leadership abilities. Aside from the fact that the beginning legal jobs that recent graduates take often don't require leadership qualities, in highly supervised settings these could even be a detriment. Any employer who did look for leadership qualities would not rely on inferences made about them from information on a resume. S/he would rely on the actual manifestation of those qualities at an interview. Applicants who list a dozen extracurricular activities on the theory that employers look for well-rounded people, might do themselves a disservice in the eyes of the employer who expects long hours of work, including evenings and weekends. Such an employer might be wary of "joiners." Or, people who list their very low first-year grades juxtaposed to their very high second-year grades — on the theory that employers like to see improvement — might not get a favorable response from those employers who expect a consistent level of high performance.

Sample resumes No. 1 and No. 2, although perhaps not the absolute last word on resumes, seem to fulfill most of the requirements of a good resume in terms of both content and form. Although these two samples contain precisely the same substantive information, they have been put together in a different style and consequently look very different from each other. Neither form is better than the other. It really is just a matter of taste.

Name. What can you possibly say about putting your name on the resume? The only problem that comes to mind involving the name occurred with a woman named "Leslie," whose resume was usually responded to with a letter that began "Dear Mr." The problem was easily remedied by adding "Ms." before her name on her resume.

Address. If you are a student and keep a residence in another place when not attending school, you might want to include both a "Local" and "Permanent" address on your resume, especially if you will be using

Contents

your resume to apply for jobs in the state or locality of your permanent address. On the other hand, if you anticipate applying for jobs in the state or locality of your law school, you might use only your local address on your resume. Many government or publicly funded positions on the state and local level will give preference to residents, and some localities even have residency requirements. For some people it would be a good idea to make up two sets of resumes — one set with just the local address and another with both the local and permanent addresses.

Telephone. Very often, because of time constraints or just plain convenience, a prospective employer will attempt to contact you by phone. For that reason you should include your phone number on the resume. If you don't have a phone, try to include some number where you can be reached, e.g. your law school. If you work, you probably will want to include both a home or evening number as well as a business or day number.

Age. Age is probably included in most resumes as a matter of course, since it satisfies the most obvious curiosity of people reading your resume — is this person 25 or 45? However, it seems perfectly acceptable to omit it, and, in fact, neither Sample No. 1 or No. 2 includes age. Although age can usually be gleaned from other information on the resume, e.g. date of graduation from college, if you feel that actually stating your age brings undue and negative attention to it, you should feel comfortable with its omission.

The arguments for and against including age as a strategy elevate the issue of age to a level of importance that is probably unwarranted. Many of the arguments are based on assumptions that can't be verified. For example, many older law students (those who did not go to college immediately after high school or to law school immediately after college) who believe their age will work against them, will often find just the opposite to be the case. Many times someone will be offered a job because their age, with its concomitants of experience and maturity, distinguish them from the bulk of other applicants.

Unfortunately the assumption that being older than most law students or recent graduates will work against you is too often correct. Discrimination on the basis of age is illegal, and therefore employers won't openly and publicly articulate their feelings. However, certain employers have often stated off the record that they would never hire someone over 35, for example. Large firms, in particular, have such an aversion. They believe older people will be unhappy and impatient working for seven or eight years towards partnership in a hierarchy that often means they are being supervised and given orders by senior associates and partners much younger than they. Whether this assumption is true or not, there is no doubt that many employers believe it and consequently are reluctant to hire older graduates.

Perhaps it is precisely for the reason that your age might work against you that you would want to indicate it on your resume! Your age will ultimately become apparent — usually at the time you walk through the door for the interview. If an employer is predisposed against hiring someone who is 45, the fact that you've camouflaged your age and gotten an interview will probably not change that predisposition. And you've probably wasted the time and effort of interviewing. Whereas if your age of 45 is stated on the resume and you still get invited for an interview, you will know that in this instance your age should not be an obstacle.

Height, Weight and Health. Despite the fact that many sample resumes include this information, it seems irrelevant to most legal jobs and need not be included on your resume. If any of these items poses a potential problem, e.g. ill health or some handicap, you probably don't want to merely mention it on a resume anyway, but would want to pursue it in detail at an interview or perhaps in a cover letter.

Marital Status. Whether you are single, married, separated or divorced is totally irrelevant to the criteria that *should* be considered in the decision to hire you, or even to invite you to an interview. Nevertheless, just as age has come to be a customary item to put on a resume, so has marital status, despite its irrelevancy. If you have no objection to indicating your marital status, go ahead. It should not have any negative consequences. But it's certainly not necessary to include it, and the assumption that being married indicates to employers that you are more stable and mature is just nonsense. Given the diversity and instability of relationships, a prospective employer would be foolish to draw any conclusions about someone's personality as it relates to work abilities on the basis of marital status.

Children. Carol Gardens, in Samples No. 1 and No. 2, does not mention anything about children just as she mentions nothing concerning her marital status. Whether or not you indicate that you do or don't have children should be completely optional.

Many women are questioned extensively about their family situation in the belief that marital and parental obligations will get in the way of their work and their career. This line of questioning, as opposed to asking about your children out of a friendly and honest sense of curiosity, should be discouraged. Therefore, you should feel comfortable about your decision to say nothing about children or other family matters on your resume.

Military Service. If you have served for a substantial length of time in the military, you might want to indicate that on the resume, if for no other reason than to account for your time. Sometimes it would be more appropriate to include this under "Work Experience" rather than "Personal Data." However, it makes no sense to indicate military status if that is merely a draft status, since no one is being drafted these days.

Photograph. There doesn't appear to be any convincing reason why a photograph should always be part of a resume. Some interviewers claim that it helps them remember someone, especially if they have interviewed a large number of people, one after another. However, it seems unlikely that an intelligent interviewer who meets an outstanding applicant will forget that candidate. Notes are usually made during or after an interview, and a person who is really outstanding will be remembered for the reasons s/he is outstanding regardless of whether a distinct facial image comes to mind.

Many employers are actually offended by the use of a photograph. They feel that the applicant is playing up to some prejudice they assume an employer has relating to physical appearance or race. If, in fact, some hirers have these prejudices, they should not be abetted in them by including a photograph on your resume.

Law School. For law students and very recent graduates who are applying for jobs, your law school and your law school academic performance are usually the items of most interest to employers. The longer you are out of law school, the less important your school and your grades seem to become, and the more important work experience looms.

Grades. Most employers are interested in how well you did in law school regardless of the differing amounts of weight different employers will give to that information. Indicate your cumulative average if to do so is advantageous. If nothing is stated about grades, most people will assume that at best you have somewhat less than a B average and are in the middle of your class. Therefore, if your average is a B or better, list it, and if your rank in class is substantially better than the middle, indicate that.

Sometimes listing your numerical average is preferable to its letter equivalent. Carol Gardens in Samples No. 1 and No. 2 is better off putting down her average as 3.2 instead of just a B. If, on the other hand, her average had been a 2.9, perhaps it would have been to her advantage to state it as a B. Sometimes an average is better than a class rank would indicate, and vice versa, and in those cases it might be a good idea to list one but not the other. For example, if Carol Gardens' 3.2 average had placed her just in the top third of her class, she might have done better to list her grades without indicating her rank. However, if a 2.7 average puts you in the top fifth of your class, it could be preferable to indicate only your rank and not your grades.

It is usually not necessary to attach a copy of your transcript to your resume. In most situations, it is never asked for, and in those cases where information on a transcript is used, e.g. by several federal agencies, forms are often provided on which to put the information that a transcript would give.

Law School Publications. Certainly, law review membership should be indicated, as should membership on any other law school publication. You should also delineate staff membership from membership on the editorial board, and list any articles you have published.

Activities. Carol Gardens seems to use good discretion in choosing to list her membership on her school's National Moot Court Team and her presidency of the Environmental Law Society. Making the Moot Court Team indicates an unusual ability relating to certain legal skills, and being president of the Environmental Law Society indicates a special interest of hers, and an interest that is probably more than fleeting. So if the guidelines are significant level of achievement or involvement, she has met them. It is doubtful that membership in a school's student bar association or participation in law school intramural sports meet these guidelines, however. To list them would not only add unnecessary information, it would also take the focus away from the more important activities that you would prefer an employer to see.

Courses. Unless you have taken an unusual concentration of courses in an area directly related to the work of the employers who will be reading your resume, there are no strong reasons for listing courses on a resume. Most people take similar courses in law school — certainly the first year — so unless you've had an unusual opportunity to specialize or to take unique courses, listing them doesn't really tell employers anything. When there are good reasons for talking about courses, it is usually more appropriate to do so in a cover letter.

College and Graduate School. The sample resumes strike a good balance in terms of the amount of information that should be devoted to pre-law school education. Once Carol Gardens has established through her grade point average, Phi Beta Kappa and magna cum laude that she did outstandingly well as an undergraduate, to have embellished that with such things as dean's list, departmental honors and other academic awards would have been senseless. In fact, she chose not to mention grades in graduate school, and this decision seems fine. After all, what's most important about her graduate studies is the field of study. You wouldn't ask someone who got a Ph.D. in Mandarin Chinese how well s/he did. Most people who get into law school these days have done very well in college, and that fact should simply be affirmed on your resume without hammering it home ten different ways.

Carol Gardens does not list any college extracurricular activities although she probably participated in at least some. However, unless those activities would have distinguished her from most other undergraduates, she was probably wise to omit them. To have listed any additional honors or activities under college or graduate school would have given more space and attention to pre-law experience than to law school itself. Since employers are primarily interested in law school, and since many law students and law graduates have been out of college for a number of years anyway, undue attention to college on the resume is really inappropriate.

High School. Why would anyone list their high school on a resume? It can't possibly be a distinguishing item. After all, we've all graduated from high school. Perhaps if you went to some private prep school and are attempting to plug into that "old boy"-"old girl" network, you would want to list that school on your resume. Otherwise, it seems superfluous.

Work Experience. Law graduates who have been practicing should give more space and attention to legal work experience on their resume than a law student. For someone who has been practicing for a while, work experience will be more a factor in evaluating that person's credentials for a job than it is for a law student. Generally, no matter what work you have done in law school — even if you've worked in one area of the law for two summers and two school years — most employers of people right out of law school look at those graduates as inexperienced lawyers who must be taught, and the salary and amount of responsibility given the new graduate usually corresponds with that perception.

This is not to say that work experience is not important information to be included on a law student's resume. It is very important, but it is important not for establishing an expertise you might have in the eyes of someone reading your resume. After all, working somewhere for two months one summer does not make you very much more experienced than someone who hasn't. Listing legal work experience on your resume is more important as a way of accounting for your time and indicating what areas of the law are of interest to you.

Prior work experience is also a way of establishing your credibility. For instance, if after working for a summer doing labor law, as indicated on your resume, you are now applying for a labor law related position, you might get more consideration than someone who didn't have that labor experience — not because you will be considered more experienced as a labor lawyer but because you have established a certain credibility regarding an interest in that field. It is that credibility, and not the experience per se, that will distinguish you from other applicants. If Carol Gardens applied for a position with a federally funded legal services program to do poverty law, she will have established her credibility as a candidate by virtue of having delineated her experience with her law school's clinical poverty law program.

Carol Gardens, in the sample resumes, chose only to list one nonlegal work experience. If you are applying for a law-related job, your law-related work experience will be of most interest to whoever is reading your resume. As for nonlegal work experiences, useful guidelines (and ones which Carol Gardens appears to have followed) are whether a particular job accounts for how you spent a large block of time, whether it was unusually interesting or unique, whether it entailed major kinds of responsibilities and whether the tasks and abilities involved relate to those that would be of interest to a legal employer. Under those guidelines, summer work as a camp counselor, salesperson in a boutique or lifeguard, for example, should probably be omitted from the resume.

The reasons why a work experience would be of interest to the person reading your resume should determine the length and substance of the job description. Carol Gardens briefly indicates the substantive areas of, her work, the tasks involved and the level of responsibility she assumed. Nothing more is needed. Many students write too much about their law clerking experiences. Most attorneys know what clerking entails — legal research, memo and brief writing, drafting non-complex pleadings and documents and doing lots of legwork. Most every law clerking job involves some variant of those chores, so it is not necessary to belabor your descriptions of those experiences. And in most cases they will be elaborated upon in a cover letter or during an interview.

Writing Sample. Even though writing ability should be something every prospective hirer would want to examine, relatively few employers ask for or read writing samples. Still, there are good reasons for listing writing samples on your resume. Aside from the fact that there are some hirers who will always want to scrutinize a sample of your writing, if writing is a strong point of yours and you have an excellent sample of your writing ability, you will want to encourage employers to ask for it — especially those who would not do so without prompting. The prompting is easily accomplished by listing the writing sample on the resume.

If you don't have a writing sample, or if the one you do have is not very good, don't say anything about writing samples on the resume. However, if you do list something, list the sample by its title. It is meaningless to say "Writing Sample — Available Upon Request." Someone intent upon reviewing your writing before hiring you will ask for a writing sample whether you offer one or not. But, by stating the title, or indicating the area of the law or the issues it examines, you might find someone who has a special interest in the subject of your research and writing, and because of that interest alone might be prompted to contact you. This is even more likely if your writing is about an unusually interesting, controversial, new or esoteric subject. Also, if the writing is defined by a title or subject area on the resume, it encourages an interviewer to discuss it with you.

Typically, the writing sample is a legal writing sample. However, sometimes it might be very appropriate to list non-legal writing. Carol Gardens' article on "The Rise and Fall of the American Automobile Tailfin" is so unique that it offers an almost irresistible cue to an interviewer to ask for it or at least talk about it. It's hard to image any interview she would have where the subject of her article would not come up. Also, since the article was published in a very respected journal, it's likely that this is the best example of her writing ability, even though it is on a non-legal subject.

The distinction between a published and unpublished work is not always so important. Your criterion should simply be whether it is a good sample — whether, if read, it would enhance your chances of being hired. In fact, some employers give less weight to published articles, since they consider them to be more an example of some editor's abilities than your own.

Miscellaneous. This is a catchall category under which to include any information that doesn't fit within the other traditional resume headings. It could include bar admissions, language abilities and interests or experiences that are unusual and will help someone in making the decision to hire you. As stated earlier, it makes no sense to list things that characterize most other people or that are totally irrelevant to the considerations of a prospective employer, i.e. common hobbies, civic activities or club memberships.

Sometimes it will be appropriate to include things under "miscellaneous" for certain employers but not for others. Therefore, different resumes may be required. Usually it's easier and more appropriate to handle this problem by mentioning the items in a cover letter but saying nothing on the resume.

References. Just as it was the case with writing samples, it accomplishes nothing to say "Available Upon Request." Of course, if someone is not about to hire you until they check references, they will ask you whom they can contact whether you offer references on your resume or not.

It's not always crucial to mention something about references since for many first jobs hiring is done without checking references. This is almost always true of summer jobs and part-time positions. However, in the case of a practicing attorney looking for another job, a job offer will hardly ever be made before a reference is contacted.

If you do have references, rather than stating "Available Upon Request," list the actual names and their place of employment. To do this is to increase the chances of giving the person who gets your resume the opportunity of connecting you to someone s/he knows. Legal circles can be quite small. List people, if you can, who are likely to have a high degree of visibility within the legal community to which you will be applying for a job. If you are applying to firms in San Francisco and can use as a reference one of your law professors who graduated from Stanford, list that person. Chances are good that a number of partners in San Francisco firms were classmates of hers/his. If someone gets your resume and sees that your reference was their old law school roommate, it is likely that that person will pick up the phone to call your reference and inquire about you. Or, someone might invite you for an interview prompted only by the nexus between you and their friend.

It is usually a waste of time to attach copies of letters of recommendation from former employers or professors. Those people who put any credence in recommendations will expect the recommendation to come directly to them from the person doing the recommending, with no one in between — certainly not the subject of the recommendation! Recommendations about you that will be given to you for copying and indiscriminate circulation will usually be written in glowing terms of generalized pap, and people who value letters of recommendation know that.

Form

The major criterion that a resume must meet in terms of its form or style is that it be readable. Readability has nothing to do with the color of the paper on which it is printed nor the cost and method of reproduction. As long as clean, clear copies are used most people don't have strong feelings about whether the resume was an inexpensive offset copy of your original — or even a good xeroxed copy — or if it was, at great expense, typeset and professionally printed on heavy bond, green paper.

Sample Resumes No. 1 and No. 2, though set up differently, would both meet most everyone's standard of readability. The information in both is presented in very clear, discrete units. It's very easy to pick out the information. Even at a glance, each school and each job stands out and can separately be focused upon. The fact that the schools and work experiences are listed in chronological order — most recent first — fulfills the expectations of most people who read resumes, and to the extent that the reader will find information where s/he expects to, readability is enhanced.

Both samples use a variety of techniques. Underlining, capitalizing or indenting all serve to focus particular attention on certain information. If these resumes used the same print throughout and used no underlinings or indentations, it would be very difficult to pick out the salient information. In addition, the net effect of using a variety of techniques is to create a resume that looks more interesting and is esthetically more appealing. Just don't go overboard. Too much variation can be confusing. Underlining everything gives the same attention to all items despite the varying levels of priority that different information should have. The most important items become obscured.

The information that Carol Gardens chose to include in her resume could not have been presented on one page and still have achieved the readability of Samples No. 1 and No. 2. A one-page resume in this case would have been too cluttered. Say what you have to say and don't overly worry about the length of your resume.

A final word about style relates to the use of complete sentences as opposed to phrases. The job descriptions of Sample No. 1 are written in complete sentences while those of Sample No. 2 are written in phrases. Either way is acceptable. The really important thing to remember is to be consistent throughout about whichever style you choose.

In Sample No. 1 Carol Gardens describes things in the first person. For some unknown reason many people seem to believe it is taboo to use "I" in a resume. It's doubtful that anyone really cares or even notices. One benefit derived from the use of "I" is that it makes sentences sound as if the person were talking, and to that extent much more of a personality seems to come through.

Sample 1

CAROL GARDENS
705 Smith Street
Brooklyn, New York 11231
(212) 437-2914

Education

HOFSTRA UNIVERSITY SCHOOL OF LAW
Hempstead, New York 11550
J.D. Expected June 1978
    Grade point average: 3.2 (4.0 = A)
    Rank: Top 15% (250 students in class)
    Honors and awards: Selected through competition to represent
      Hofstra on National Moot Court Team
      President, Environmental Law Society

UNIVERSITY OF WISCONSIN
Madison, Wisconsin 84502
M.A. in Urban Studies, June 1972
    Honors and awards: Recipient of full tuition scholarship and
      teaching fellowship

STATE UNIVERSITY OF NEW YORK AT STONY BROOK
Stony Brook, New York 11783
B.A. in American History, June 1971
    Honors and awards: Graduated magna cum laude, Phi Beta Kappa
      History prize as top-ranking student

Employment

ROPER & GRAY
25 Broadway
New York, N. Y. 10007
Summer 1977
    As a summer associate I was involved with research and
    memoranda writing on a number of cases that were being liti-
    gated by the firm. Since the firm has primarily a products liabil-
    ity practice, my research was done in that field.

COMMUNITY LEGAL ASSISTANCE CORP.
73 Main Street
Hempstead, N. Y. 11550
Fall 1976
    As a second-year student I worked in the Neighborhood Law Of-
    fice, which is the Law School's clinical poverty law program. I
    was responsible for handling a number of civil and criminal
    cases in all their aspects except court appearances.

Employment
OFFICE OF THE DISTRICT ATTORNEY
155 Leonard Street
New York, N. Y. 10013
Summer 1976
>As a summer law intern my responsibilities included interviewing witnesses, field investigations, legal research, preparing motions and memoranda and courtroom observation.

CITY OF NEW YORK DEPARTMENT OF CITY PLANNING
2 Lafayette Street
New York, N. Y. 10007
1972-1975
>As a city planner for the City of New York, I had major responsibility for the planning of the Clinton District Urban Renewal Project, primarily in regard to environmental aspects.

Published
Article
"The Rise and Fall of the American Automobile Tailfin,"
Journal of Popular Culture, Spring 1973.

References
Professor James Purdy
Hofstra University School of Law
Hempstead, N. Y. 11550

Professor and Associate Dean Alice Stern
Hofstra University School of Law
Hempstead, N. Y. 11550

Mary Gladstein
Associate Director
N.Y.C. Department of City Planning
2 Lafayette Street
New York, N. Y. 10007

Sample 2

CAROL GARDENS
705 Smith Street
Brooklyn, New York 11231
(212) 437-2914

EDUCATION: Hofstra University School of Law, Hempstead, New York 11550
J.D. Expected June 1978
Grade point average: 3.2
Rank: Top 15% (250 students in class)
     Honors: — Selected for National Moot Court Team
              — President, Environmental Law Society

University of Wisconsin, Madison, Wisc.
M.A. in Urban Studies, June 1972
     Honors: — Recipient of full tuition scholarship and teaching fellowship

State University of New York at Stony Brook, Stony Brook, New York 11783
B.A. in American History, June 1971
     Honors: — Graduated magna cum laude
              — Phi Beta Kappa
              — History prize as top-ranking student

EMPLOYMENT: Summer Associate — Roper & Gray
                      25 Broadway
                      New York, N. Y. 10007
                      Summer 1977
Researched and wrote memoranda on a number of cases being litigated by the firm, primarily in the field of products liability.

Student Intern — Community Legal Assistance Corp.
                  73 Main Street
                  Hempstead, N. Y. 11550
                  Fall 1976
Law School's clinical poverty law program. Was responsible for handling a number of civil and criminal cases in all their aspects except court appearances.

EMPLOYMENT: <u>Summer Intern</u> — Office of the District Attorney
                                 155 Leonard Street
                                 New York, N. Y. 10013
                                 Summer 1976
                Interviewed witnesses, did field investigations, did legal research,
                prepared motions and memoranda, and observed trials.

                <u>City Plannner</u> — City of New York Department of City Planning
                                 2 Lafayette Street
                                 New York, N. Y. 10007
                                 1972-1975
                Had major responsibility for the planning of the Clinton District
                Urban Renewal Project, primarily in regard to environmental as-
                pects.

PUBLISHED   "The Rise and Fall of the American Automobile Tailfin,"
ARTICLE: Journal of Popular Culture, Spring 1973.

REFERENCES: Professor James Purdy
                Hofstra University School of Law
                Hempstead, N. Y. 11550

                Professor and Associate Dean Alice Stern
                Hofstra University School of Law
                Hempstead, N. Y. 11550

                Mary Gladstein
                Associate Director
                N.Y.C. Department of City Planning
                2 Lafayette Street
                New York, N. Y. 10007

Cover Letters 3

The cover letter that is sent with the resume can often be more important than the resume itself. The fact that much less space is devoted to a discussion of cover letters than to resumes, or that no sample cover letters are provided, does not reflect the degree of importance that should be given to the cover letter. It simply reflects the fact that there are less constraints on writing cover letters than on resumes: they cannot be discussed as definitively nor illustrated adequately by samples.

Cover letters should write themselves. Whatever the reasons are for sending a resume, the cover letter articulates them. Are you inquiring about a part-time job, a summer internship or a full-time position? Are you writing because you know about the place by reputation, you read about it somewhere or someone recommended it to you? Are you writing to find out about a job opening or merely to set up an interview to get information?

The reasons and circumstances for sending a resume are infinite, and therefore the content of the cover letter has few boundaries. Also, the stylistic "rules" for writing cover letters are much more open-ended than those for writing resumes. Cover letters have neither a prescribed length, nor an optimal number of paragraphs, nor a recommended sequence of information.

<table>
<tr><td>PURPOSES</td><td>Cover letters do what resumes cannot. Most people make up a general resume, i.e. one that is written to be sent to a number of different places within a range of varying legal work settings. The cover letter has the major function of making this more or less general resume specific to a particular kind of work setting and a particular person or place within that type of setting. Individualizing a resume through a cover letter is accomplished by elaborating upon certain items in the resume, emphasizing certain other bits of information and adding information that is not mentioned in the resume at all.</td></tr>
</table>

Carol Gardens only mentions in her resume that she worked for a firm that handled products liability cases. If she sent her resume to the United States Consumer Product Safety Commission, she probably would want to elaborate in her cover letter on the exact nature of the cases she worked on, the exact level of responsibility she assumed, and how her experience working for a firm led to her decision to apply to a federal regulatory and enforcement agency.

She might want to emphasize her work in the law school's clinical poverty law program, because it was in dealing with poor clients that she first came in contact with people victimized by defective products. Carol Gardens might also want to add the fact that she took courses in torts, products liabilities and consumer protection. She should also add that she did an independent study project which entailed doing a paper on a products liability issue.

Individualizing the resume for the Consumer Product Safety Commission makes her a stronger applicant than if her applicancy stood on the resume itself. This Commission receives hundreds of unsolicited resumes each year, so individualizing, and thereby strengthening, her resume becomes imperative.

In a certain sense a cover letter is really an expedient. It obviates making up a different resume for each place you apply to. The information that is appropriate for one place, but inappropriate for all other places, is easily dealt with via a cover letter. The fact that you speak Spanish and lived in Spain for six months might be irrelevant to every place you apply to except the one firm that has a large number of Spanish-speaking clients. Or, you might not want to take up space in your general resume to mention where you grew up and lived prior to college, and where you still maintain some indices of residency. However, this information becomes very relevant if you are applying for a position as a legislative aide with the congresswoman who represents that district. In both these examples, what was irrelevant information for most prospective employers — and therefore was not on your resume — is very relevant and appropriate information to recount in your cover letter.

A major benefit of individualizing or personalizing a resume by the use of a cover letter is the enhancing of your credibility as an applicant. By relating how you came to apply to a place, recounting all the things you know about its work, and matching that work with your interests and background is to establish your application as a credible one. That is, by so doing, you show that your resume has not been sent out randomly or that this organization is only one of a hundred to which you have sent it. In a tight job market it is crucial that you give the recipient of your resume the feeling that it has not merely been dredged up in a dragnet.

Cover letters that say little more than that your resume is enclosed usually arise from random, mass mailings and a basic ignorance about the places that will be receiving your resume. And, if you are writing to places far outside the range of your credentials and experiences, it also becomes impossible to say much in the cover letter. In both instances any cover letter is useless since is can't individualize and consequently won't help to make you appear as a strong and credible candidate. Although it is easy to understand the job hunting anxieties which produce mass mailings, you should avoid them as much as possible. Perhaps it can be a last resort, but under no circumstances should anyone *begin* to look for a job with blind, indiscriminate mass mailings. It is definitely worth the effort to figure out, within some limits, what you want to do and to find those places to which both your interests and prior experiences relate.

Another thing that a cover letter enables you to do is to convey much more of your personality than a resume. The cover letter is you talking in complete sentences. It is you developing and presenting ideas in an ordered way. It is much closer to you as you might sound in a conversation. To the extent that it reflects more of you as a personality, it gives an employer more reasons to see you. If ten people with equal credentials, as portrayed in their resumes, are being considered for a job, and only three can be asked to Washington, D.C. for an interview, personality factors — whom would I *like* to meet — assume a greater importance.

Cover letters can give the person who receives your resume several options. In a cover letter requesting an interview, you can leave the initiative with the prospective interviewer or take it yourself. In writing to an out-of-town place, you can mention the dates you will be in town and ask for an interview during that time. Alternatively, you can suggest the possibility of meeting somewhere inbetween that city and your own. Or, you can ask if some business trip to your area is planned in the near future — at which time an interview can be arranged. If a job opening is not available, you can ask to meet to discuss job prospects or job-hunting techniques in general within that particular legal setting or geographical area. If someone can't be positive about your resume, ask them to pass it on to some other place. In other words, give the person as many options for responding positively as possible. The cover letter can set up these alternatives, a resume by itself cannot.

Finally, it might even make sense for some people to use a letter in lieu of a resume. An unusually skimpy resume can give a negative impression. If you find yourself in the position of having only enough information to fill half a page of a resume, rather than sending a half-page resume, simply incorporate those few items of information into a letter. Very often a first-year student, who has come to law school directly from college, will have nothing relevant to offer in a resume for a summer position besides that s/he graduated college and will have completed one year of law school. These two items of information can better be conveyed in the context of a letter. A resume is not demanded in every situation.

Always address your cover letter to some person. Ideally, you will have selected a person for very specific reasons, and in that situation there is no problem. However, you will often be writing to a place for specific reasons but will not know the most appropriate person there to receive your resume and cover letter. *Try to find out!* If the most appropriate person gets your materials your chances for getting a positive response increase. Also, sending your cover letter to the right person further establishes your credibility. One regional counsel for a federal agency mentioned how impressed he was when an application was sent to him personally. Since he was not so visible, it meant someone did some

ADDRESSING THE COVER LETTER

research, and the research meant that the applicant was probably very interested in his agency and was not merely applying to every federal agency hoping to find some job somewhere. All other things being equal, that's impressive.

The problem of sending the cover letter to the right person is manageable when you are writing to a fairly limited number of places. It becomes very problematical when you do mass mailings. No one can call 500 firms to get the names of hiring partners. However, even if you can't find the most appropriate partner, it is better to send your resume to some partner rather than to just the firm. Without having empirically tested the assumption, it has always seemed that there is a better chance of getting a positive reply if your cover letter and resume catches the eye of a partner rather than a receptionist. Instead of testing out this theory, you would do better to limit the places to which you apply, establish the reasons you are applying to these places, and direct your application to the right person — someone you have gone to the effort of finding out about.

| **REPRODUCING THE COVER LETTER** | Many of the same problems that relate to addressing cover letters apply to reproducing them. Again, if you are dealing with a limited number of places, the ideal of individualizing and typing each cover letter is attainable, but if you are writing to a massive number of places, it is not. |

Mass-produced cover letters broadcast the fact that you are blanketing the market, and that fact can only affect a recipient of your application in a negative way. No one likes to feel as if someone has applied to them simply because they want any job anywhere.

If absolutely forced to engage in a mass mailing, as a desperate last resort, then do it in a way that will broadcast that fact in the least blatant manner. Xeroxed or offset printed letters addressed to no one or no place and that begin "Dear Sir/Madam" are perhaps the most blatant method. Subsequently typing the name and address onto mass-produced cover letters is the second most undesirable way (especially if the print types don't match). Perhaps the most preferable way of mass-producing cover letters is to have them done on an automatic typewriter which has the original letter on a magnetic tape and the name and address is typed in manually. But even this method broadcasts a mass mailing, for although the letters have been individually typed they have not been individually composed, and this will be obvious. One letter cannot possibly appear personalized when its contents attempt to speak to 500 different employers.

Even if you are doing a mass mailing with a reproduced form letter, whenever you are able to individualize in the context of that mailing, do so. If out of 500 places you know something about 20 of them, at least don't send your form letter to those 20.

Interviews 4

"Of the people I interview, 25% are axed as soon as they walk through the door. I would never hire anyone who was fat or had acne, nor would I hire any guy who had blood on his collar from shaving."

A hiring partner
in a medium-sized law firm

Interviews vary greatly in their importance to the final hiring decision. At one extreme is an employer like the Justice Department which will hire law graduates for their prestigious Honors Program on the basis of one 20-minute interview. At the other extreme is the ten-attorney firm that will make someone a job offer only after that applicant has been interviewed by every partner and associate in the firm, a process that might take the better part of two or three days (including lunches).

The importance of the interview seems largely a function of an employer's capacity to accommodate different abilities and personalities. Large institutional hirers like the Justice Department or the very large corporate law firms can make use of a wide range of skills and personality types. A smaller organization, however, has much more narrowly defined needs, and those needs must be met by someone with particular skills and whose personality will fit in.

Of even greater variation is what actually comprises "the interview." There are very few accurate generalizations that apply to all interviews regarding their length, style or subjects of discussion. Also, there is no ideal way an interviewee would conduct her/ himself, since that ideal changes with every interview, depending on the different kind of work setting and who is doing the interviewing. In fact, most of the observations in this chapter relate to the pitfalls of looking at interviews normatively — thinking they should be a certain way.

Interviewing should not be thought of as a game, which, if you learned how to play it well, will lead you to fame and fortune. On the contrary, a gamesmanship approach to interviewing might win you a prize — *a* job or *some* job — that you would do better without. The fantastically high attrition rate amongst recent law graduates, in terms of their first jobs, attests to this.

It's important to be honest and straightforward about the kind of job you're seeking and about yourself as a person. You can't expect to be liked by everyone who interviews you. Nor should you try to be. If you are hired by people who are attracted to you for what you *are* and not for what you *can be* at an interview, you are more likely to find work that is satisfying and people you enjoy.

Finding places that do the kind of work you're most interested in and people you are apt to like is also the best preparation you can have for an interview. Common interests will ensure the best interviews. When you're sincerely interested in a job, and your background and credentials support that interest, you will never have to think up appropriate questions to ask the interviewer — they will come quite naturally. Not only will these interviews be exciting and even enjoyable, but they'll produce job offers.

Interviewing for jobs about which you know a great deal and in which you have a keen interest should be the ideal. Anything less is a compromise. If the compromise is because of the exigencies of a tight job market, it is one thing. If, however, it is a result of your laziness concerning what you want to do and where you want to be, it is another matter.

Preconceived Notions of a "Good" Interview. There is no predictable posture or subject of conversation that will serve you well at all interviews. A firm handshake, a smile, lots of eye contact and five good questions are not the key to interviewing success, despite what articles on interviewing say. Rather than going into an interview with a game plan, you should be open and responsive to each interviewer and to the unique dynamic that s/he will create with you.

SOME COMMON PITFALLS

There is no right amount of aggressiveness to display. Some interviewers expect to do most of the talking and will like you only if you portray yourself as a good listener. Other interviewers enjoy the ease of interviewing someone who takes all the initiative and does most of the talking. Similarly, there are no ideal questions that should be asked in every interview. Asking questions for the sake of asking will often come off as stilted and simply unresponsive to the situation. Questions that you should know the answers to, especially if already given in the course of the interview, could be fatal. Standardized questions often just sound silly. Depending on the context, asking a prospective legal employer about legal research facilities might be as credible sounding as the college applicant inquiring as to the number of volumes in the library!

No boundaries are placed on what can be discussed at an interview. The appropriateness of different subjects merely changes from setting to setting and from interviewer to interviewer. There are some things that are very likely to be discussed at most interviews — anything that is on your resume; your law school (how you like it, why you chose it and what other schools did you get into); your faculty; your grades (or some reference to your academic performance); prior jobs you've held; and why you are applying to this particular place. However, outside this fairly obvious range of subjects, you can expect anything. Most interviewers are looking for bright and articulate people whom they like, and almost any topic allows an interviewee to reveal those qualities. You can talk about the weather or the latest Supreme Court decision. Non-legal subjects can give clues to your abilities as a lawyer as easily as legally related topics. Talking in a conversational style can be as informative of your knowledge and skills as answering hypotheticals or playing devil's advocate.

Perhaps the most prevalent criticism interviewers have made is that interviewees don't allow interviews to happen. Because of rigid styles, prepared questions and rehearsed answers, they do not engage in the normal give and take that characterizes most successful social interactions.

Monolithic View of Lawyers. Related to the problem of looking at interviews as predictable or definable experiences is the problem of narrowly viewing the legal profession and lawyers. The mass media, law schools and our own image of how we would like to be have all contributed to this. All lawyers are not the same!

The woman who bought herself one, all-purpose

interviewing dress found herself overdressed at many interviews. A law student who cut his hair prior to his interview with a prestigious Wall Street firm was quite surprised to find one senior partner's long grey hair pulled back and tied in a ponytail. Equally surprised was the orthodox Jewish student who, after long debate, decided not to wear a yarmulke to his initial interview at a firm and discovered the partner who interviewed him was wearing one.

Passiveness. Most interviewees are passive, not in the sense that they don't talk a lot or don't speak forcefully, but in the sense they are basically responding *to* the interviewer. They are asked a question and they answer. They don't participate at all in setting the tone or in choosing what gets discussed. They don't give *and* take. They only give.

One consequence of merely answering questions asked of you, is that you reveal things about yourself without offering any opportunity for the interviewer to be revealing. Interviewers have egos and therefore love to talk about themselves as much as anyone. Talking about one's self or about one's interests is usually an enjoyable experience, and in the context of interviewing, enjoyment is often synonymous with a good interview. An interviewer spent a day at a law school interviewing third-year students. His interviews consisted of asking each student the same two hypotheticals. Every student, but one, reported how awful their interview was. The hypotheticals were silly and unanswerable, and the interviewer was so somber and serious. The one exception reported that her interview consisted mostly of the interviewer talking about his banjo playing. Somehow she had got him onto that subject. Needless to say, the interviewer reported that she was the most impressive student he had interviewed that day.

Most interviews, to repeat, *can be* conversational.

Although sometimes an interviewer will contrive the situation and set things up just to see how you react — drawing an X through your resume as you sit down or posing a hypothetical and then ticking off the 30 seconds s/he gives you to come up with an answer — most interviewers do attempt to conduct an interview in a conversational manner.

Defensiveness. Certain questions tend to put interviewees on the defensive — what other law schools did you get into (if this happens to be the only one that accepted you); what are your grades (if they happen not to be particularly noteworthy); or how did you do on the LSAT's (if your score was not very high). There is no right answer to these questions. However, if any of these or other matters will be predictably problematical for you, make sure that however you deal with them at an interview, don't be defensive or apologetic.

One of the things that many interviewers forget (especially older interviewers) is that it is much more difficult to get into law school these days than it was when they applied. LSAT scores that got someone into Yale 20 years ago might not make them a viable applicant at any law school today. So, interviewers should be made aware of the changing circumstances and should not be smug about their own past academic achievements. One applicant for a judicial clerkship was asked by the judge why, if she had done so well in college, she chose to go to law school where she then was. Since the judge taught at that school on an adjunct basis, she answered by asking him why, if he was such an outstanding judge, he chose to teach there.

Selling Yourself Only. It isn't a good idea to think of interviews as opportunities only for you to induce a hirer to make you a job offer. Even in a tight job market, you have to make intelligent choices about job offers, and there is no better opportunity to get information about a place than the interview.

Contrary to a lot of the literature that enumerates the do's and don'ts of interviewing, there should be no subject that is taboo for you to broach at an interview, assuming it is of genuine concern to you, and you can ask it tactfully. For some reason it has been assumed that it is taboo to ask questions about salary at a first interview. This presumably indicates that you're more interested in the money than the work itself. This seems like nonsense. To ask about salary does not indicate that money is your all-consuming interest in the position. Since everyone expects to be paid for their work, an employer would probably think it very curious if an applicant *didn't* ask about salary.

Not Realizing Limitations of Interviews. Interviews perform their function most effectively when "all other things are equal." If you have an interview with a place that has never hired anyone who was not an editor of law review, and you have grades that rank you in the bottom of your class, your interview is likely to be useless if you expect from it serious consideration for a job. If a public defender's office never hires anyone who hasn't had extensive criminal law trial experience, you would be frustrating the utility of an interview (as well as yourself), if absent any criminal law experience at all you interviewed for the job.

There are a lot of people who believe that if only they can get their foot in the door, by dint of personality they'll get the job. This is usually true only if you have the other objective credentials the employer demands of all viable applicants. Not only is it frustrating to interview for a job that under no circumstances could you be offered, but it wastes time and energy that can be used to interview for jobs that you are qualified for — jobs that don't require your bowling people over with your personality.

Interviewing for Practice. Most people get better at interviewing as their confidence about it grows. However, that confidence will grow only as a result of positive interviewing experiences. For that reason it makes no sense to interview — just for practice — with those places you know nothing or little about, are not interested in, or don't have the barest of credentials that would make you a viable candidate. In each of these situations the chances of having a positive experience are reduced by what you bring, or don't bring, to the interview. It's doubtful that a series of "practice interviews" where there was very little common ground, lots of lulls in the conversation, embarrassed answers to questions about credentials, and no job offers would make someone a better interviewer. On the other hand, interviewing for jobs for which you have a strong interest and excellent credentials is likely to give you feedback that can profitably be translated to other interviewing opportunities.

Related to this is the problem (especially of law students during the so-called fall recruiting season) of going on too many interviews within a limited space of time. Going on ten interviews in the course of a week will not be good practice. Without the enthusiasm and freshness that usually go along with good interviews, overdosing on interviewing is not a good idea. Pacing is important.

Interviewing for a Job Only. Interviews have multiple purposes. Though typically people interview at a place for a job opening they know to exist, it is often useful to interview for the purpose of gaining information about finding a job — within a particular field or in a geographical area. As long as both you and the interviewer are clear about the purpose, these interviews can be fruitful.

It might be a waste of time for someone at the bottom of the class to interview for a job at a place that hires only law review editors. However, it might not necessarily be a waste of time to interview with an attorney there about possible job-hunting strategies, people to contact, ways of bolstering your credentials and part-time or volunteer opportunities. So, if immediately after starting an interview you scheduled a month ago you are informed that the position that was open has just been eliminated by a budget reduction, all is not lost. Don't leave that office without a list of 15 other places to contact that do the kind of work you're interested in. Let people help you.

In short, given the generally high level of competence that characterizes law graduates, employers are much less likely to make a wrong hiring decision than are lawyers likely to accept the wrong job. To minimize the chances of making bad decisions, it is necessary to squeeze out every bit of information at an interview that you'll need in order to make intelligent choices. The choice does not always have to be between two or more job offers. Unless your financial vulnerability dictates otherwise, there is still the choice of taking a job or not even though there is no other immediate alternative position available to you.

Although the exact nature of what will transpire at an interview can never be predicted, there are some useful generalizations to be made about interviewing for particular types of positions. These can never be used as an absolute guide — and the exceptions will be numerous — but they can, nevertheless, offer some perspective about interviews in different work-settings. Also, the

SOME OBSERVATIONS ABOUT PARTICULAR WORK SETTINGS

generalizations should reinforce the fact that the needs of different work-settings often require that interviewing be conducted in different ways.

Law Firms (Large). These are the corporate firms with recurring hiring needs for both full-time and summer positions. These firms typically fill their openings through a fall recruiting program entailing on-campus interviewing at some number of law schools. More so than any other type of employer, these firms uniformly place great emphasis on academic credentials — your law school (how prestigious) and your grades (how good).

Because of the focus on school and performance, the function of the interview is more limited than in those situations where non-academic criteria are given more consideration. More people are eliminated by large firms before they walk in the door — on the basis of school and/or law school grades — than by any other legal employer. Interviews tend to be very chit-chatty and topical. This is true of both the initial "screening interview" (if the firm recruits on-campus) as well as the "call back or office interview."

Since many of the large firms are competing against each other for the same people, their interviews become an integral part of a total recruiting program through which they attempt to sell themselves. Visiting law schools all over the country, flying applicants in for interviews and lunches at expensive restaurants are all part of this recruiting effort. The interview itself is just another part of it. Many students have commented that their experience interviewing with large firms conjured up images of fraternity or sorority rushing.

Also, large firms are able to use people with different skills and personalities in many different capacities. Therefore, it is less important for the interview to elicit what smaller places would deem to be important personality or character traits. In fact, a few years ago approximately 80 firms agreed to take through a lottery, sight unseen, one Harvard law student for the summer selected at random!

Large firms can also accommodate hiring mistakes more easily than small employers. In fact, large firms depend on their attrition rate to enable them to hire the ten, 15, or 20 new associates they take on each year.

Law Firms (Small). These can include single practitioners or firms of 30 attorneys. However, they all share the trait of having limited hiring needs and placing considerable emphasis on non-academic factors in filling those needs. Usually a position has to be filled by a particular kind of person who has fairly specific abilities that the firm requires. Most small firms cannot hire the person who is a brilliant brief writer only.

The following example of how one firm conducts its interviews is reflective of the needs — and their fulfillment through interviewing — of a number of other small firms. This particular firm has a profile, or a sense of its own ambience, and looks for people who meet it. "We are looking for a little spark. People we will like and in whom our clients will have confidence. We're looking for a partner. We're looking for ourselves."

This firm will have the interviewee talk about some legal subject. It is, hopefully, a subject about which the interviewer can play devil's advocate since there is, then, a discussion as opposed to the applicant merely expounding.

In addition, the interviewee will be asked to respond to some unexpected non-legal question. Often this firm will ask, "If after five or six years in our firm, you wake up one morning, look in the mirror and say there is a successful lawyer, what would you have had to accomplish in those years to make that statement?"

Or, "What abilities or attributes do you have that will make you a successful lawyer? And what flaws do you have that might prevent you from being a successful lawyer?" Or, "Do you believe you have to be on your way to becoming a partner to feel you are a successful lawyer?" Or, "Do you feel you have to do pro bono work to consider yourself successful?"

Since small firms have more at stake than large firms — hiring mistakes are more problematical — more weight is placed on the interviewing process. (Despite the huge amount of time large firms expend on recruiting, time spent is not necessarily synonymous with importance.) For this reason, small-firm interviews often are more probing, more substantive and less chatty than those at large firms. In addition to the interview, small firms will often read writing samples and check references before a job is offered, whereas large firms will almost never do so, at least for a new associate's position.

Government. Since people are generally less informed about the legal work of government agencies and the role of government lawyers compared to private firms and private attorneys, government interviews are often characterized by the spending of a lot of time talking about the work of the agency. In fact, most of the comments heard about interviewers monopolizing the interview pertain to government interviewers.

At least in terms of federal agencies, the question of what the agency does is obscured by the large size of many of the offices within the agency employing lawyers. Different divisions or bureaus within the Office of General Counsel, for example, will have very different functions from each other, and this takes explaining. The problem of "what do you do" becomes even further complicated on the federal level by the fact that regional offices often have much different responsibilities than the Washington, D.C. office. So, many an interview is spent in describing those distinctions as well.

Since it is often the case that someone who has applied to one government agency is applying to several other agencies — federal, state or local — interviewers will always attempt to find out if you have a particular interest in their agency or if it's just one of 20 you've applied to. Therefore, when applying to any government agency be prepared at the interview to establish the legitimacy of your interest in that office.

With the exception of the Justice Department, offices of state attorneys general, and county or city attorneys' offices, most government agencies do not do litigation. Perhaps, since litigators are not being sought, the qualities of a litigator do not have to be elicited at interviews. This might account for the fact that, as a rule, government interviews tend to be much less "set up" or contentious than many firm interviews or the interviews of prosecutors' or defenders' offices.

Corporate Legal Departments. In several respects the circumstances that surround interviews with a government agency are similar to those that characterize interviews with the legal department of a corporation. The work of the corporation lawyer is even less visible and less known than that of the government lawyer. Consequently, interviews become opportunities for interviewers to both explain the legal department's work and extol its merits. As a way of explaining the information-giving tenor of corporate interviews, remember that these offices also do very little litigation. There is no necessity for probing those personality traits that presumably make up a good litigator.

Topics you can expect the interviewer to bring up would be, among others, the distinction between what legal work the corporation does in-house and what it has done by retained outside counsel. The function of the legal department within the total corporate structure must be explained. It is usually necessary to discuss the involvement of the corporation's lawyers with business as well as legal matters. Also, what mobility, if any, is there from the legal department to management positions?

Criminal Defenders' and Prosecutors' Offices. Since these offices are primarily hiring litigators, they place heavy reliance on the interview to reveal those qualities they feel a good litigator should have. Typically, those qualities include such traits as sensitivity, persuasiveness, flair and the ability to think on your feet. Objective credentials give very little insight into these qualities; interview is the best vehicle for assessing them.

The following example of how one criminal defender's office conducts interviews, even though it doesn't characterize all legal aid or public defenders programs, should be instructive. Since this office is looking for people who will be litigators, it will ask applicants questions to see how they think and react to unanticipated situations. In assessing their responses the interviewer looks for directness, sincerity, salesmanship and style. Carefully formulated questions are posed to discover if an applicant has rigid attitudes or if s/he is "self-oriented" as opposed to "client-oriented."

In addition to general questions about criminal law and the criminal justice system — what interests you, what attracts you, what repulses you — hypotheticals such as the following are asked:

"You are assigned to represent a defendant who has been charged with raping a young child. Your client has admitted his guilt to you. Could you persuade a jury to acquit your client?"

"You are assigned to represent a defendant charged

with throwing hot ashes on children. After giving one story to you and another to the fire marshall, s/he asks you what story you would suggest for the trial. What do you say?"

"You represent a defendant who has admitted her/his guilt to you but refuses to accept a plea. You go to trial on the defendant's word that s/he won't commit perjury. During the course of the trial the defendant decides to take the stand and commit perjury. What do you do?"

There are no right answers to any of these questions. But what you say, and the way you say it, will give clues to what you think, how well you think, how much interest and thought you've devoted to criminal law, and what your attitudes are about practical ethical problems you would have to grapple with on a daily basis.

The following example of how one district attorney's office conducts interviews reveals that prosecutors utilize interviews in similar ways and for similar purposes as defenders.

This particular office looks for people with "a sensitive heart, a thoughtful mind and a combative spirit." To glean these qualities any question, legal or non-legal, that can be thoughtfully responded to is asked. Any non-legal question can work as long as it doesn't rehash the resume. What books have you read recently? Which writers do you like? Why did you choose a city law school rather than a campus school?

This office will explain the realities of the job and will want to know how an applicant reacts to them. "What do you think of a criminal justice system that prosecutes only a very small percentage of those who are indicted?" "How do you feel about putting people in jail?" "How do you feel about police?" "What are your feelings about prostitutes?" "What do you think of wire-tapping as a means of getting evidence?" "How do you feel about the death penalty?"

This office will ask an interviewee how s/he feels about prosecuting certain kinds of cases. "Could you prosecute someone for possession of marijuana?" "Do you feel any differently about prosecuting for white collar crimes as opposed to street crimes?"

Invariably, this district attorney's office will ask questions that will examine your ideas about prosecutorial discretion. "You have been assigned a case and you're only 50% convinced of the defendant's guilt. Do you prosecute that case or do you get it dismissed?" "In that same case would your decision be affected by whether or not there had been a grand jury indictment?" Aside from finding out what a person thinks, these kinds of questions enable interviewers to determine if someone is merely giving answers they think the interviewer wants to hear. "We want to find people who are independent minded, but who are not arrogant. If someone is arrogant, they will be arrogant in court, and they will also be arrogant about someone's guilt or innocence."

Often, the interview in both defenders' and prosecutors' offices — especially after an initial screening — is conducted by a panel of two or three attorneys. Aside from it allowing more people to see a candidate, it is thought to provide a better opportunity to see how candidates handle themselves in the more pressured setting that the panel creates.

Judicial Clerkships. Perhaps more so than for any other position, the interview is crucial in getting a clerkship. The success of a clerkship, both from your viewpoint as well as the judge's, depends on your abilities to work together. This is especially true of trial court clerkships. The skills that are required of a clerk are fairly well defined and can usually be determined from paper credentials and recommendations. Therefore, the interview serves only to determine whether the judge likes you and would like to work with you.

Beyond some predictable questions about why you would like to clerk, why you chose that court and why you chose that judge, there are few guidelines. One person got a clerkship with a judge on a state's supreme court after an interview that consisted of a four-hour dinner in a restaurant on a Sunday evening!

Private 5
Firms

"Two attorneys can live in a town where one cannot."

Proverb

Dear Mr. Ms. ———:

I am in receipt of your letter to my partner inquiring into the prospects of a summer clerkship with us next summer. Over the years it has become apparent to us that a certain level of academic attainment is a requisite to satisfactory performance with us. Furthermore, we have over the years hired most of our summer clerks from a group of law schools known to us where we were familiar with the levels of academic attainment. We conduct interviews on campus at those schools and thereafter further interview only a small fraction of those students at our offices.

Although we occasionally interview in our offices students from law schools other than those in the above group, we find it necessary to confine such interviews to a very small number in order not to overburden the recruiting personnel and not to conduct interviews where there are no realistic prospects of our making a job offer. Therefore, even though we consider many non-academic factors which contribute to the development of a competent attorney, I do not believe it would be meaningful for you to schedule an interview with us since we have already interviewed or have scheduled this fall a number of applicants with truly superior academic records who would, I believe, receive preference in our selection process for the few positions we have to offer. We therefore believe that your scheduling an interview with us would constitute an unwise investment of time and effort on your part.

Thank you, in any case, for getting in touch with us.

Very truly yours,

(An actual form letter sent by a firm in response to a student's resume and cover letter)

The two major problems people encounter in looking for jobs with law firms are *where* to look and *when* to look. Some firms (primarily large corporate firms) prepare firm resumes or other descriptive materials for use during the fall of each year when they fill full-time and summer positions. The firms recruit through law school placement offices, either through on-campus visits or the solicitation of resumes. However, despite their visibility, these firms account for only a small fraction of the job offers that are made to law students and graduates nationally. The bulk of law firm offers come from those firms (primarily small general practice firms) about which there is scant information. These small firms have unpredictable hiring needs that are not announced and filled through any one source such as law school placement offices, private personnel agencies or particular publications. Other than *Martindale-Hubbell*, where do you find lists of firms and information about their type of practice? Do you apply to these firms during the fall or spring or after you graduate?

This chapter discusses various strategies for approaching the private firm job market. It also lists and describes those resources that can be used as a way of supplementing *Martindale*. These resources will not usually reveal listings of job openings per se. Rather, they will lead you to people and places that might have a job available, but more likely will be a source for finding additional contacts. Finding an opening often depends on just being lucky. By pursuing different strategies and by writing and talking to lots of people you will be creating a certain momentum, and that momentum will increase your chances of being lucky. Also, since jobs are found in many different, often unpredictable, ways, it is reasonable that they be searched for using a variety of methods.

Aside from the fact that *Martindale* is not an all-inclusive listing of firms, it is important to go beyond it, since it tends — like placement board notices, prepared lists in placement offices or newspaper ads — to funnel applicants to the same places. In seeking out other less obvious or conventional sources, you are likelier to find job openings that 400 other applicants haven't also discovered. Also, the way you discover a place becomes the basis for your cover letter: you are writing to a particular firm because someone you talked to recently had recommended it, or, you attended a conference and the firm was mentioned by several of the panel participants, or, a newspaper article indicated that the firm was handling a case in the area of law that precisely coincides with your field of major interest. In other words, the way you find a firm becomes the way of indicating that you have a good reason for contacting it. That reason establishes your interest and your credibility — certainly compared to other unsolicited applicants.

The same sources that ultimately will lead you to job openings, are also the sources for your learning what kind of practice a particular firm has, or, more generally, what it's like to practice in a certain field of law, in a large or small firm, in a specific geographic area, in the city or the suburbs or in a general practice or a specialty.

This search will also make you aware of certain options — types of law that are practiced — that you probably had never thought about.

In conducting your search for a position with a private law firm, always be aware of timing. With the exception of the large corporate firms whose hiring needs account for the phenomenon of "fall recruiting" (filling predictable job openings almost a year in advance), very few firms hire in advance of the time that they actually need someone. Most firms could not begin to accurately respond to a third-year student's inquiry about a job upon graduation if made several months prior to that time. In fact, the needs of most small firms are such that when they need to hire someone, it is usually necessary for that person to be able to actually practice, including making court appearances. Therefore, it is more likely that small firms will be responsive to your job inquiries if made after you have graduated or passed the bar and been admitted.

Unfortunately, fall recruiting has prompted the widespread belief that the best people get the best jobs several months before they graduate. Aside from the deep anxiety this creates for those people who don't have offers before the end of the school year, it induces students to have unrealistic expectations and to look for jobs prematurely. A third-year student in October sends off 200 resumes to medium and small firms, gets only 25 replies and only one interview, and is demoralized by the lack of response to the large mailing. S/he exclaims, "The job market for lawyers is unbelievably tight." Actually, the response to the mailing is less reflective of the job market than it is of bad timing, or of false expectations.

This is not to say that it is a complete waste of time to write to smaller firms some months in advance of the time when you can actually start working. There *are* some firms that can — and will — hire in advance, and the only way to flush them out is to write early. If from writing to 200 places you get one interview and one job offer, you haven't necessarily wasted your time. Also, by writing early you will often get responses that you can follow up several months later. Just be realistic about what the response can be, and don't write a place off simply because six months ago you had written and gotten either a negative response or none at all. If you make overtures to firms at one point, and are still looking several months later, retrace your steps.

There could be many reasons why your letter was not answered, so don't read that much into a no-response. In addition — and this is more likely to be the case — the hiring needs of a firm can change from one day to the next. You write to a three-attorney firm where there is no opening and your resume gets thrown away. Four months later an associate leaves that same firm and there is an opening. Your follow-up to that firm might coincide with that associate quitting. For that reason — and especially if you have a particular interest in a firm — a second overture four months later makes sense.

You are not a failure if you don't have a job offer by December 15 of your last year in law school. Most graduates of most law schools don't find their jobs until after they graduate. In addition to the unnecessary aggravation the "December 15" mentality creates, it works towards cutting off some potentially quite useful sources of job information, i.e. other students and faculty. Because many students are reluctant to share their "failures" with others, they do not talk about their job-hunting problems. Therefore, they forego the possibility of letting others be helpful. Students especially pick up all sorts of job information and leads that they could share. In one instance a student was seeking a job with a midwestern firm where he could use his foreign language ability. His interests were quite unique. He found such a place when another student, who was aware of his interest, came across such a firm in his own job-hunting travels and told him about it.

Have faith that all jobs are not filled by December 15. Even the large firms that recruit during the fall sometimes hire people late in the school year or after graduation. Either they did not fill all their positions through fall recruiting (not everyone who gets an offer takes it), or they will simply hire one more person. A firm will not let an outstanding applicant go by merely because s/he applied out of the so-called hiring cycle.

---

*RESOURCES
Directories

Martindale-Hubbell Law Directory. The problems in using *Martindale* arise because it provides only limited information about firms, and it leads people to write to the same firms as everyone else who uses it. If two people are interested in applying to firms in Atlanta that do tax work, they will both turn to the biographical section of Atlanta firms, flip through looking for taxation under type of practice and come up with virtually identical lists of 30 or so firms. Because of this "funneling" process, it is not uncommon for firms listed in the biographical section to get hundreds of unsolicited resumes each year. For those firms listed in the most sought-after geographic locations, i.e. New York, Boston, Washington, D.C., San Francisco, the applications sometimes number in the thousands.

The biographical section is a paid-for listing of

*Most of the printed materials cited in this and succeeding chapters are readily available and can usually be found in a law school placement office or law library. Many of the materials can also be obtained from the reference section of a public library. For those who wish to order their own copies, all materials cited are listed, after the last chapter, along with the name and address of the publisher.

firms, and for that reason only a very small percentage of the total number of firms that exist in any geographic area get listed. The firms listed in this section under Santa Fe, New Mexico, for example, might account for only about 10% of all the law firms in Santa Fe. Also, the information in this section is limited to a brief characterization of the type of practice (very often stated simply as "General practice"), a listing of partners and associates with biographical data about them (i.e. date and place of birth, college and law school attended with graduation dates, bar admissions, publications and honors), and sometimes a listing of representative clients. Because of the limited extent of the listings and the amount of information given, *Martindale* should certainly not be looked at as the only, or even the best, source for finding firms to contact. It should be used as a starting point, or a supplment, or, in certain circumstances, a last resort.

As a starting point you might want to write to the labor law firms listed in *Martindale* in a particular city requesting an interview to discuss labor law opportunities in that area and, if possible, to get names of labor firms not listed in *Martindale*. Or, as a law student in Texas you might want to write to general practice firms in Northern California to arrange appointments to discuss the viability of a recent graduate from out-of-state starting her/his own practice there.

As a supplement, you might turn to *Martindale* to get some information about a firm mentioned in a law article that was of interest to you — to find out its size, type of practice and the name of someone at the firm you could contact. Perhaps you've come across the name of an attorney who serves on a bar association committee that addresses itself to the area of the law in which you're interested. In that case you could use *Martindale* to find the firm the attorney is with and some confirming information, e.g. has this attorney published anything that coincides with the area of law that the bar committee is concerned with or does the firm's type of practice coincide with that area?

As a last resort — when you feel you've exhausted all other leads and methods and can't think of another place you could possibly write to — you might find yourself using *Martindale* to compile a list of firms for a large, non-selective mailing. This is not a recommended thing to do, but despite all the caveats against it, it's certain that some students and graduates will do mass mailings anyway. So, at least if you are going to risk the effort and expense of this unendorsed method, don't limit yourself to the back, biographical section of the directory. *Martindale-Hubbell* also has a front section! This is a fairly comprehensive listing of attorneys and firms in any area, though it doesn't give the biographical information or the type of practice characterizations that the biographical section does. Nor can you always tell the size of the firm. However, it does give the age, college, law school and date of admission for each lawyer listed, and by going down the listing under a geographic area you can often get a sense of the size of a firm by the number of times you see it listed next to the names of attorneys. As for type of practice — at least for most single practitioners and small firms (especially small suburban firms) — the firm is probably engaged in some variant of a general practice. Remember, this is a last resort, and in this context using the front section — however scanty the information it provides — is certainly better than limiting yourself to the firms listed in the biographical section. Also, however little information you can glean from the front section, it is more than you can get from a listing of lawyers and law firms in the yellow pages of a phone directory, which many people do use for compiling lists of places to contact.

Since these mass mailings are not very selective, there being no particular reason why you are writing, and since there will be very little you can say in your cover letter to establish your interest or credibility in writing to a firm (you probably will have, in fact, resorted to form, mass-reproduced cover letters), at least try to address your letter and resume to someone in the firm likely to be more responsive to you than anyone else at that same firm. Although this requires a lot of guesswork, there are some common sense guesses that can make your mailing a bit less random.

In selecting the person to write, look for affinities with you or your law school. Certainly write to alumnae(i) of your college or law school. Write to someone who graduated from a law school the same year as a dean or faculty member now at your law school. If a dean or faculty member at your law school taught at another school for a period of time, write to an attorney who is likely to have been taught by that person. These match-ups are even better if the potential connection is also someone you list on your resume as a reference.

All of the affinities stated thus far can be established from the front section of *Martindale*. If a firm is also listed in the back, biographical section, additional items can be examined. Did an attorney serve on the same law review as someone on the faculty of your law school? Did someone write articles or serve on committees that relate to your interests and background as they are portrayed in the resume that person will be getting? Sometimes prior places of employment will be indicated in the biographical information. In such instances try to establish whether a faculty member or a reference of yours worked with that person. Did you ever work there yourself? Partners are better to write to than associates. As for younger partners over older ones, it's anyone's guess as to who is likely to be more responsive.

Bar Association Directories. Bar associations at all levels — national, state and local — publish annual directories that contain very useful information for someone trying to figure out which firms to contact. The primary value of all these directories for the job hunter is the breakdown of the bar association's committees with a listing of each committee's members. These committees are typically organized on the basis of substantive areas of the law, and the members are usually attorneys who practice in that area.

Therefore, these committees and their members can be sources for learning about opportunities in general in that field of law, and, more specifically, for getting names of other lawyers and firms in a particular locale that practice that type of law. Obviously, some people will be more willing than others to provide information, but from this pool of attorneys, defined by their interests and expertise, it is certainly likely someone will help you by offering some job-hunting strategies as well as specific places to get in touch with.

For example, from the *Directory of San Francisco Lawyers* you can get the name, address and phone number of a lawyer on the labor, criminal, international or admiralty law committee. Contacting someone listed in *The Association of the Bar of the City of New York Year Book* as a member of the standing committee on copyright, entertainment, environmental or tax law might be a very good way of getting some leads to firms practicing in those fields of law. Especially within narrow fields of law or within specific locales, people in a field know everyone else in that same area of practice. Contacting, and then meeting, a member of the Santa Clara County Bar Association's Matrimonial Law Committee might be a far superior way of finding divorce lawyers in Palo Alto, California than simply going through *Martindale-Hubbell*.

The *American Bar Association Directory* gives addresses for many state, city and county bar associations around the country. In addition, you can count on just about any locality having its own bar group. Although some associations might be reluctant to make copies of their directory available to non-members, there usually are many ways of finding a copy, e.g. local law libraries and practitioners in that locality.

The ABA *Directory* (which can also be found in Volume VI of *Martindale*) is itself an excellent source for finding attorneys who specialize in a particular field. Members of each committee of the ABA are identified by the state where they practice. So, if you're interested in practicing customs law in Los Angeles, and a member of the Customs Committee is from Los Angeles, s/he is a logical person for you to write or call.

Using bar association committee members as sources of information can be particularly helpful if you are interested in an esoteric area — especially a field not delineated in *Martindale*, such as children's rights, law of the mentally disabled, energy law, consumer law or housing and urban development law. It is also very useful if within a fairly broad field of law, you are interested in a specialized aspect. The ABA *Directory*, for example, breaks down the Labor Relations Law Section into various committees such as union administration and procedure, arbitration and collective bargaining, unemployment benefits, workmen's compensation, pension law and occupational safety and health law, to name but a few of the divisions. The *Directory* also lists any newsletter or other publications a committee publishes, and these offer additional sources of information and leads in that field of law.

Finally, beyond the leads that these bar association directories might give you, browsing through the committee structure (especially such a detailed organization as the ABA's) will often give you ideas about certain areas of practice that simply had never occurred to you before. For instance, you might never have thought of the enormous scope of administrative law practice until you discovered the almost 50 substantive committees of the ABA's Administrative Law Section.

Other Directories. There are all sorts of directories that have been compiled for specific areas of practice. Whatever the field, these directories can guide you to firms within it. And they can point you to people who can be helpful. The *Directory of Opportunities in International Law* is an excellent starting place for anyone who wants to compile a list of firms that have an international law practice. *Who's Who in Labor* might put you in touch with some prominent labor lawyers who would be willing to share information with you. Looking under "litigation" in the *Women's Organizations and Leaders Directory* might yield the name of a woman attorney who would be responsive to your questions about job hunting as they relate to you as a woman law student or law graduate.

The directories that will be of interest to you depend upon what you're looking for and where. A good book to go through in search of directories that might be relevant to your needs is the *Guide to American Directories* — a directory of directories! Look under the heading of "Legal" or "Labor" or other substantive areas.

Professional Associations

There are numerous organizations of lawyers that have been created to pursue certain common interests. Sometimes that common interest is a substantive field of the law as is the case with the following associations: American Academy of Matrimonial Lawyers, Association of Immigration and Nationality Lawyers, International Law Association, Association of the Customs Bar, National Association of Criminal Defense Lawyers, American Patent Law Association or the Maritime Law Association of the United States.

Often the common interest is something other than

a substantive area of practice such as in the following groups: National Association of Women Lawyers, National Association of Black Women Lawyers, Puerto Rican Bar Association or the American Association of Attorney CPAs. Try to find organizations whose interests coincide with your own, whether those interests are substantive or something else. Then make overtures for suggestions, information and leads. Many associations have directories of members which they make available.

Sometimes, the more specific or esoteric your interests, the easier it is to find groups that can be directly responsive to them. The American Blind Lawyers Association, for example, has a small constituency whose members are well known to each other. The services it provides and the functions it fulfills are well defined. Someone who shares the problems and interests of this group and plugs into its network is likely to get very useful information.

It is relatively easy to find associations that could be helpful to you. Two excellent sources are the *Encyclopedia of Associations* and *National Trade and Professional Associations of the United States and Canada and Labor Unions*. Both these publications provide basically the same information — name, address and phone number of the association; the name of the executive director; and items relating to membership, staff size, publications or newsletters, and conventions or conferences. Also, since many of these associations are national organizations, they will often be located in Washington, D.C. and can be found in publications dealing specifically with Washington such as *Washington IV*. This book has a section titled "Lawyers Associations." Or, you can even get a copy of the District of Columbia yellow pages and go through the listings under "Associations." Over 1500 associations are listed in the Washington yellow pages.

Conventions and Conferences

Bar associations and other professional groups of attorneys hold annual conventions and meetings as well as sponsor, on an ongoing basis, various conferences, workshops, speeches and symposia. Although some of these activities might be foreclosed to non-members, it is possible to attend many of them if an overture to the right person is made and the strength of your interest is established. These events provide opportunities for meeting people who are apt to share your interests and be knowledgeable about a field of law, including job possibilities within it. Also, lawyers will often be much more accessible in these settings than they are in their offices. Demonstrating your interest by attending a program might elicit a much more personal and helpful response than would your unsolicited resume sent to a lawyer's office — especially if s/he was inundated with applications.

Finding out about the occurrence of conventions or the topics of talks should not be a problem. Various publications related to the interests of a group will publicize events. The *Encyclopedia of Associations* and *National Trade and Professional Associations* indicate newsletters put out by a group, and these will announce programs. These same two publications also indicate whether an organization holds a convention or meeting on a regular basis, and sometimes will even give the date and location of the next one scheduled.

Continuing Legal Education Program Brochures

A very good way of supplementing the list of attorneys and law firms in a particular field compiled from *Martindale* is to get hold of the brochures that announce the programs run by various bar continuing education groups. These programs are organized around areas of practice or issues, and the attorneys who conduct the workshops or seminars are experts in their fields. The program brochures list the attorneys who will participate in a program and usually identify them by their place of employment. By going through current and back issues of these brochures, you will discover people and places you simply would not come across in *Martindale* or elsewhere.

Different groups in each state usually run their own programs. The New Jersey Institute of Continuing Legal Education (ICLE) and California's Continuing Education of the Bar (CEB) run programs in their respective states, for example. On a more national basis, the Practising Law Institute (PLI) and the American Law Institute (ALI) conduct nationwide seminars throughout the year.

PLI, for instance, conducts almost 300 seminars each year. Many of the seminars center on general areas of the law such as: Securities Law, Personal Injury Law, Law, Federal Tax Practice, Estate Planning, Criminal Defense, Collective Bargaining and Arbitration, Trademarks, Patent Law, Anti-trust, Federal Civil Rights Litigation, Corporate Litigation or Real Estate. Other seminars are about very specialized types of practice such as: Ocean and Coastal Law, Commodities and Futures Trading, Legal Problems of the Record Industry, Representing the Professional Athlete, Legal Aspects of Doing Business in East Asia, Counseling Clients in the Entertainment Industry, Medical Malpractice, International Taxation or Defending White Collar Crimes.

It is often possible to attend these seminars. Although there is a fee for those who attend, sometimes an accommodation will be made for a student by providing a "scholarship" or reduced rate. And even if you can't attend, the seminar publications still provide an invaluable resource.

Each of the almost 300 seminars run by PLI annually has a program brochure or newsletter that lists the faculty that will run the workshops. Writing to PLI to request back issues and to get on their mailing list is a particularly good idea as the brochures provide an invaluable source of leads in terms of identifying people in particular fields of law. And of course, these people in turn could lead you to others in that same or related area. This is especially helpful for specialized areas of interest, for although *Martindale* might help you find entertainment firms, it won't identify those lawyers who specifically represent record industry clients. Or, it will indicate criminal law firms but not firms that represent white collar criminal defendants in particular.

Publications   *Newspapers.* It is hard to imagine any copy of a major newspaper that will not have several references to lawyers and law firms. For that reason, you should read the paper with an eye to looking for job leads. Articles about criminal cases or investigations will identify the attorneys involved. Articles reporting labor disputes often identify the lawyers or law firms representing the various parties. Announcements of government appointed panels will list the members, who will often be lawyers and will be identified by the place of employment. New appointees to various industry and governmental positions will often be lawyers, and their firms will be mentioned. In addition to articles, leads in newspapers lurk in other contexts — in letters to the editor, editorials and even obituraries and wedding announcements.

It might be a good idea to go through *The New York Times Index* looking under such headings as "Legal Profession," "Crime," "Labor," "Anti-trust Actions," "Bankruptcies," "Wills and Estates," "Courts," "Law and Legislation," "International Law," "Divorce" or "Taxation," to name some of the more obvious possibilities.

Many of the larger cities have newspapers that just

report legal news, such as the *New York Law Journal* or the *Los Angles Daily Journal*. Although these papers have job opening listings (mostly for experienced attorneys to fill immediate openings), their primary value to a law student or recent law graduate lies in their providing leads to lawyers who might be able to give you information. These papers are filled with articles about various legal subjects written by attorneys identified by their expertise and place of work. Other articles will make reference to lawyers and firms in a specific context. The *New York Law Journal* once ran a series of articles about practicing law in the suburbs in the New York City metropolitan area. Those articles were based on interviews with attorneys who, along with their firms, were cited. It provided a wealth of information not available from *Martindale-Hubbell*.

Specialized Journals and Law Reviews. If your interests are in a clearly defined area of the law, go to the journals concerned with that area. These journals consist of articles written by practitioners in the particular field, and these authors are always identified by where they work. An article offers a perfect reason for making an overture to someone, especially if you have a credible interest in it or it relates to research and writing you yourself have done. A few of the specialized journals that could be helpful to those whose interests correspond are the following: *Arbitration Journal, Journal of Taxation, National Journal of Criminal Defense, Securities Regulation Law Journal, Anti-Trust Law Journal* or *Bulletin of the Copyright Society*.

Law review articles can provide the same leads. For both law reviews and specialized journals, go through the *Index to Legal Periodicals* under subject headings related to your interests, make a list of articles and journals, and then start browsing.

General Legal Periodicals. Juris Doctor magazine and the *American Bar Association Journal* both publish articles about a broad spectrum of issues and events in the legal field, as does *Case and Comment*. Go to a law library and skim through back issues of legal periodicals and you'll be amazed at the ideas that will come to you in terms of people you can contact and different types of practice.

Bar Association Journals and Newsletters. All bar associations publish something, ranging from very thick journals filled with excellent articles to three-page newsletters that do little more than list events and summarize disciplinary actions taken against attorneys. Most will provide you with hints — names of lawyers and law firms; recently published articles, magazines and books; and scheduled meetings, conventions, talks, special programs and seminars.

Alumnae(i) Publications. Undergraduate schools publish alumnae(i) journals of some kind. A college's alumnae(i) news will report on graduates, class by class, and you can count on the fact that scores of these graduates have gone on to become lawyers. These publications offer a good way of finding people who, because of your ties to the same school, are likely to be responsive to your inquiries. Some undergraduate schools even prepare a separate list of their graduates who have become attorneys (perhaps for fund-raising purposes), and might share the list with you.

Law schools also publish journals which include alumnae(i) news. Sometimes' it is profitable to go through issues from a law school other than your own. Although lacking the affinity that will exist between you and a graduate of your own school, you can still get good leads to lawyers and firms that practice the kind of law in which you're interested. Many law schools, in addition, publish almnae(i) directories which provide information about all living graduates of that school. Aside from guiding you to graduates of your school, these directories can be used to discover firms that historically have been receptive to hiring graduates of your law school. They can be particularly helpful if you are looking for people to contact in other parts of the country. If you can find three graduates of your law school who are willing to talk to you about legal opportunities in Denver, you've got a good start on researching that job market.

Books. Outside Counsel: Inside Director delineates those law firms that have a member sitting on the board of directors of a corporation which the firm represents. The book is of some use to the job hunter, for it enables you to identify the kind of practice of certain firms by the corporate clients they represent. From the nature of business of a corporate client, you can determine that a law firm has an international, anti-trust, entertainment, aviation or admiralty practice, for example. However, since most of the corporations are large, their law firms are usually among the major corporate firms, and therefore most of the same information can be obtained from *Martindale*. Nevertheless, the book is still worth reading, for there are some very interesting exceptions to this.

Although the following books will not necessarily give you leads to people or places, they are good books for learning about what certain types of practice are like. *Practicing Law in New York City* contains some very good articles about different firm practices. Even though the articles are by lawyers who work in New York, what they have to say about large, medium or small firm practice is relevant to other cities. For those comtemplating setting up their own practice, *How To Go Directly Into Solo Practice Without Missing a Meal,*

How To Start and Build a Law Practice and *I'd Rather Do It Myself* might all prove helpful.

Placement Services and Agencies

Most bar associations and professional organizations for lawyers operate some kind of placement service, ranging from those that function by word of mouth to those that employ full-time staff and are quite systematic. However, even the more systematic and most successful of these services are not likely to be that helpful to the law student or the very recent law graduate. These programs are most useful to the practicing attorney with a specific kind of experience, for the typical employer that will use this kind of placement service is one with specialized hiring needs that are not likely to be met through law school placement office listings or from unsolicited resumes. For those places that hire recent graduates, law school placement offices and the unsolicited flow of resumes that inundate most firms provide an adequate enough pool of applicants, and a further listing with some other placement service is unnecessary.

What has been said about associations' placement services applies also to private placement, or personnel, agencies in terms of students or inexperienced graduates. Private agencies do a lot of placement for experienced attorneys in corporations. Even the law firm placements are primarily for positions that require a number of years of a specialized experience. In addition to these constraints, private agencies tend to be oriented to the very prestigious law school.

None of this is to say that association and private placement services are entirely useless for all but the experienced attorney. However, in using these sources be aware of their limitations, and, as should be the case with all resource alternatives, do not use any one avenue to the exclusion of others.

Pursue all the ways suggested in this chapter. Job offers come about in many, and sometimes strange, ways. Interview as many people as possible and stimulate momentum. A job will come, and probably in a way that you could never have predicted.

Government 6

" . . . citing his experience as an agribusinessman the President suggested that the Secretaries reduce the size of their departmental legal staffs whose oceans of paperwork, he said, have been a persistent irritant to him and probably issued from the lawyers' lack of anything else to do."

> *President Carter addressing*
> *his Cabinet, as reported*
> *in The New York Times — Jan. 1977*

FEDERAL GOVERNMENT

Although job applicants tend to look at "federal agencies" as a single entity, the reality is that there is a startling absence of uniformity in the way that different agencies fill their job openings for lawyers. In some agencies the hiring responsibilities are centralized, and one office does the hiring of lawyers for all divisions and branches within the office of general counsel or solicitor. In other agencies the different divisions have great autonomy in filling their own staff openings. Often, personnel offices staffed by non-lawyers have a major role in the hiring of attorneys for an agency though in most cases lawyers themselves handle the

85

administrative functions involved in hiring other lawyers. In some agencies Washington does the hiring for regional offices. In most situations, the regional counsel or solicitor makes employment decisions independently of Washington. Some agencies fill positions months in advance through active recruiting programs. Others hire only when there is an immediate opening and rely on unsolicited applications.

It is imperative that you learn and understand the distinct needs and procedures of each agency to which you apply. Failure to do this will make many of your applications futile. It would, for example, make little sense to send your application to the Office of General Counsel of HUD in Washington, D.C. if you were interested only in the Kansas City regional office. Or, your chance for serious consideration might be greatly reduced if you apply to the IRS Chief Counsel's Office in May of your third year of law school, since that office tries to make offers soon after its fall recruitment program is finished.

Identifying those agencies that hire lawyers is a relatively easy matter. What is much more problematical is finding the right person, or best person, within an agency to whom to apply. In fact, most of the resource listings in this chapter attempt to help in solving that particular problem.

Despite what many government prepared publications might say, avoid sending an application for an attorney position to a personnel office. Many agencies — especially the larger and more visible ones that have active recruiting programs — have offices, staffed by non-legal personnel, to handle much of the administrative duties involved in processing a huge number of applications. Although some of these personnel offices are quite conscientious in processing and circulating applications, many become cemeteries for massive numbers of applications. This seems to be particularly true of those agencies that recruit on-campus at certain law schools. Applications from people at schools other than those visited tend to be directed to personnel or administrative offices where they are buried.

It's a better idea to send your application to a lawyer within the general counsel's or solicitor's office who is integral to the hiring process. Often this will be a deputy general counsel or deputy solicitor, or an executive assistant to the top legal officer of the agency. In those agencies where each division has a certain amount of autonomy in hiring, it makes sense to apply to a division head or branch chief, especially if your interests and background are well defined and coincide with the work of a particular division within the office of general counsel. If your application is destined to wind up in personnel, it will get there no matter where you send it initially, but at least a lawyer might look at it who has distinct hiring needs and credential requirements, and who will be in the best position for matching them with you. In fact, sometimes it's good strategy to send more than one application to an agency. Send one to the office of the solicitor and two others to two different division heads whose divisions do work of interest to you. Three separate applications that are initially seen by three different people might increase the chance that the best person will get to see your application.

Another major problem in looking for a job with the federal government is the timing of the application. Some of the larger agencies try to compete with the major corporate firms by predicting their attrition and hiring people in advance through fall recruiting. Most of the legal departments of executive agencies make offers several months in advance of the time an applicant can begin work. Some of these include the departments of Justice, HEW, Treasury (IRS), Interior, HUD, Labor and Transportation. Several of the independent agencies fill positions in advance as well. Some of these agencies are:

the Federal Trade, Communications and Power Commissions, National Labor Relations Board, Environmental Protection Agency, Energy Research and Development Administration, General Accounting Office, General Services Administration, SEC, Interstate Commerce Commission and the Postal Service. However, most federal employers of attorneys do not hire in advance, but rather fill an opening only when it actually becomes vacant. This is almost uniformly true of all regional offices, even in agencies where the Washington, D.C. office hires well in advance. Regional offices are relatively small and attrition is minimal compared to Washington. Therefore only a handful of regional offices are ever in a position to make prior commitments based on predictions of vacancies.

When, then, is the best time to apply to federal agencies? If you are a third-year student, you should apply in the fall of that year to those offices that engage in fall recruiting. For other agencies, it is also a good idea to apply in the fall as a way of making an initial contact or inquiry, but make sure you reapply or reactivate your application later in the year — and again after you graduate if need be. If you are a graduate and are ready to commence work immediately, apply anytime and hope that your application coincides with someone's quitting.

Certain agencies won't hire in advance because they simply don't mobilize to make attrition predictions and recruit. Since agencies can make a fairly accurate prediction of their budget and staff size for a given fiscal year almost a year in advance, the only real variable *is* attrition. However, most agencies won't make prior commitments because their small size makes such offers based on predicted attrition too risky. These agencies are often extremely desirable places in which to work, and their inability to make you an offer early in your last year of law school should not in itself dissuade you from pursuing a position with them. If you really want to work for the Equal Employment Opportunity Commission (EEOC), you must resign yourself to the fact that you probably will have to wait until near or after graduation before you can receive an offer. If a position with the EEOC is important to you, you would be making a mistake to accept a position with another agency simply because that agency made you an offer in December of your last year of law school.

A good time to apply or follow up on applications with agencies is towards the end of each fiscal year. Near the end of each fiscal year (September 30) an agency is likely to know if any money is left in that year's budget which can be used to fill staff needs. Also, agencies will want to be at their staffing limit at the fiscal year's end, because to operate below the budgeted staff size for the year might indicate to those reviewing the next year's budget that the agency could function adequately with a staff size smaller than the level requested. Not only will budget matters be clearer for many agencies around the late summer-early fall, but this is also the time when many people make career moves, so attrition might be greater at this time. (Even though an attorney with some years of experience quits, that position is still very often filled by someone at the entry level.)

The problem of timing (the gap between when an application is received and when the position is filled) points up another matter, namely, the need to aggressively pursue and follow up on applications once they have been made. This becomes even more imperative given the numbers of applications each agency gets and the form procedures many agencies have created to handle the deluge. Below is an actual letter sent by one agency to its hundreds of applicants, a letter very typical of what you can expect of several agencies. It reads:

Dear Student:

I have received your letter of inquiry relative to a position with this office for employment after you graduate.

I am unable to state what our requirements will be at this time, but I will retain your correspondence and review it when we will better know our needs and authorizations. This should occur in May.

You will be notified in the event that you are selected for an interview.

I appreciate your interest in this Department.

Sincerely,

Regional Counsel

This form letter is usually sent in response to what is a form application, i.e., Standard Form 171, your resume and perhaps a supplemental application that an agency prepares for attorney applicants. How does one transcend the forms, the numbers and the fact that positions are often filled months after your application is submitted? In a word, be aggressive. Or, as one person who handles recruiting for the solicitor's office of a federal agency put it, "Worry me to death until I get tired of you."

It is simply not enough to send in your application and leave it at that. Especially where an agency has had your application for a long time, follow it up with an updated resume or a letter giving new information and expressing your continued interest in that agency. Many agencies, when they actually start reviewing applications for a vacant position, will not consider stale resumes. Often times an agency, faced with hundreds of applications accumulated over the months, will have no idea who is still interested. Indicating that you are still interested will give you a distinct advantage over the hundreds who don't. Since so many people blanket agencies with applications, your continuing contact indicates that your interest in that particular agency is probably more than just an interest to get *some* legal job with *some* agency in Washington, D.C.

Go to Washington. Interviewing at the agency increases your chances for distinguishing yourself from other applicants and is a way of showing your strong interest. Agencies are, uniformly, more likely to hire someone they've interviewed than someone they've not.

If you've applied to the Washington office, go to Washington. If you've applied to a regional office, interview in that region. If you can't make it to Washington, interview at a regional office and have them forward their recommendations to Washington. Or perhaps someone from Washington will be coming to a regional office where you could meet them. Suggest these alternatives to Washington when you apply. Sometimes one regional office will even do interviewing for another regional office. In all cases interviews are crucial, *so get interviewed*. Even if you've been interviewed on-campus, it is sometimes a good idea to get to see additional people by visiting the agency.

It is relatively easy to see people at agencies, and very often advance notice or scheduled appointments are unnecessary. Offices in Washington, D.C., especially, are used to having applicants from out of town come through, and will therefore try to accommodate "off the street" visits. Some agencies, in fact, have a panel of lawyers that meets on a regular basis for the sole purpose of interviewing applicants who come to Washington.

Interviewing at agencies will lead you to people and information that you would otherwise never find out about. There is an extensive grapevine of information in Washington, and finding people who are part of that grapevine could lead to unique opportunities. This is particularly true in regard to legal positions other than in agencies. Many "Hill" jobs (i.e. legislative aides or assistants and congressional staff and committee positions) become known and get filled through word of mouth.

Before listing the resources available for use in seeking legal positions with the federal government, some mention should be made of the distinction between attorney positions and quasi-legal jobs. Federal attorney positions, which at the entry level pay GS-9 or GS-11, are excepted from Civil Service competitive examination requirements. However, there are a number of quasi- or para-legal positions such as law specialist, hearing and appeals examiner or investigator, which at the entry level pay GS-5, GS-7, or GS-9, and are filled through The Mid-Level Examination and the Professional and Administrative Career Examination. Although these positions are often less challenging and pay less than attorney positions, in a tight job market hundreds of law students and graduates have sought them.

Those jobs that are filled through the Mid-Level Examination are probably of most interest to lawyers. These would include para-legal specialists, hearing and appeals examiners and tax law specialists positions with such agencies as Justice, HEW, IRS, Interior, Transportation, Environmental Protection Agency, General Accounting Office and the Civil Service Commission. (The publication *Federal Career Directory*, put out by the Civil Service Commission, gives a good summary of these positions.) After completing the Exam (which is an examination of your credentials rather than an exam as such), you are placed on a register, and from that register lists of certified candidates — in order of rank — are sent to agencies as they have positions to be filled. Agencies must hire from the top of the list. However, since an agency can request to have someone placed on the certified list and then, on the basis of interviews, decide not to hire those above that person on the list, there exists a certain amount of latitude to work towards a particular person. Because of this control and because the positions pay GS-9, the Mid-Level Exam might be worth your investigation. It is about five months, at the earliest, before you can expect to be hired once you've completed the exam. Therefore, it would make sense to complete it around February of your third year, so the earliest possible hiring date will coincide with your availability.

Those quasi-legal positions filled from the Professional and Administrative Career Examination (PACE), such as investigators and benefit and claims examiners, require taking an actual exam, the raw score from which determines your ranking. Agencies hire on the basis of these scores alone. Since you would have very little control over what agency you would work for and since the pay is hardly comparable to attorney positions (either GS-5 or GS-7 and, in fact, most PACE Exam jobs are filled at GS-5), it's difficult to be enthusiastic about this option. Also, as regards both the Mid-Level and the PACE Exams, preference points are given to veterans, so either option becomes less attractive to non-veterans.

Of General Information. The single best source of information pertaining to legal positions with the federal government is *Federal Government Legal Career Opportunities*, published annually by the Law Student Division of the American Bar Association. This book lists the offices which are the major hirers of lawyers, and for each office there is a summary of information regarding the number of anticipated openings in the next year and a half; the total number of lawyers presently employed by an agency; where the legal positions are located

**RESOURCES
Directories**

(Washington, D.C. only or in the regional offices as well); entrance pay levels and qualifications; a description of the nature of the legal work; and application procedures.

Although this book is the logical starting point for anyone seeking an overview of legal opportunities with the federal government, it should not be used as your sole source of information. Many of the descriptions of the nature of legal work are too brief or too general, and therefore are inadequate. Also, too often the structural breakdown of an office into its divisions and branches is oversimplified, and thereby neither the complexity nor the breadth of the legal opportunities are accurately portrayed. (These deficiencies can usually be made up by obtaining the literature from an agency that specifically describes the work of that agency's legal department. Also, the *United States Government Manual* is a good supplemental source of information.)

Its major failing, however, is that it steers all applicants to the same places. Not only does it direct people to the same agencies, but it directs all applications to *an office*, e.g. the office of general counsel or the personnel division (sometimes the personnel or administrative office is for the entire agency and not for attorney hiring only). Rather than sending an application to the office of the general counsel, it is often useful to send an application to, or meet with, a particular person within an agency who does precisely the kind of work you're interested in. Therefore, the following list of directories will be for the purposes of helping you understand the organizational structure of a legal department with its various divisions and subdivisions and helping you find attorneys within those departments with whom you might have an affinity by virtue of common work interests or for other reasons. As it was stated earlier, people are sometimes impressed that you had the interest and did the research to discover them.

Of Organization Structures. The most detailed organizational breakdown of a legal department is provided in the telephone directories of agencies. Each agency has its own telephone directory which is also an organizational listing. These directories can be obtained from the Government Printing Office for about $2 to $4. They are often printed quarterly so the information is very current. Or, instead of purchasing them, when you visit Washington, plan to spend a few hours in a Government Printing Office Bookstore. Go through the telephone directories of various agencies and pick out those people you would like to contact (addresses, room numbers and phone numbers are provided).

Whereas *Federal Government Legal Career Opportunities* lists only the general heading of "Office of the General Counsel" for HEW, and directs all applications to "Executive Assistant," the *Department of Health, Education and Welfare Telephone Directory* gives a complete breakdown of the General Counsel's Office. From this breakdown you discover that the General Counsel's Office consists of the following divisions: Business and Administrative Law, Civil Rights, Education, Food and Drug, Legislation, Public Health, Human Resources and Social Security. You also discover the various branches, and their chiefs, within each division having responsibility over litigation, contract, compliance or legislative matters, for example. You therefore have a much better picture of the scope of the legal activities of the office, and you have the names of people whom you can contact and who are more likely to be closer to your interests than the "Executive Assistant." Also, lawyers within the different divisions are likely to be more approachable than some one administrative official.

An additional benefit you receive by going through an agency's phone directory are ideas about where in an agency other than in the office of general counsel or office of the solicitor, lawyers might be employed. You will discover administrative law judges, examiners, commissioners and appeal board members who often have clerks who are attorneys. You will discover offices for congressional affairs, legislation, civil rights or consumer affairs, all of which might be interested in someone with a law degree.

If you are applying to a regional office, a regional telephone directory will serve you well. Usually there is one directory for a region which includes all the agencies in that region. Although such a directory is not available to the public, it is possible to go to any regional agency's office and ask to look at the directory. Sometimes the telephone directories for the Washington, D.C. office will include information about its regional offices, but this is not usually the case.

More readily available, though not as detailed as the agency phone directories in their organizational breakdown, are the *Congressional Directory* and the *United States Lawyers Reference Directory*.

Perhaps an even better source than these two directories is *Martindale-Hubbell*. Although most people use *Martindale* primarily for getting information about private attorneys and law firms, its separate "U.S. Government Lawyers Section" (following the front section for the District of Columbia) is an excellent guide to the organization of legal offices, as can be seen from the table of contents for this section. *Martindale* lists all offices within an agency that employ lawyers — not just the office of general counsel or solicitor. You see under Department of Commerce that in addition to the Office of the General Counsel, Economic Development Administration, Maritime Administration and Patent Office (the only employers of lawyers indicated in the book *Federal Government Legal Career Opportunities*), lawyers also work for the National Bureau of Standards, National Fire Prevention and Control Administration,

National Oceanic and Atmospheric Administration and the National Technical Information Service. *Martindale* also lists all lawyers who work on the staffs of the Senate or House, on congressional committee staffs or as aides to senators or representatives.

By glancing over an agency's listing in *Martindale*, you can quickly get an idea as to the number of lawyers an office employs; where lawyers are distributed among the various divisions; which divisions seem to hire recent law graduates; and patterns, if any, of the kind of schools from which an office or division seems to hire.

A major advantage of *Martindale* is that it enables you to find lawyers with whom you, might have an affinity by virtue of schools they graduated from. You can find lawyers who graduated from the same school as you or from the same law school the same year as a faculty member you know willing to make an overture on your behalf. Washington, more so than any other place in the country, is populated with lawyers who grew up and graduated from schools in all parts of the United States. At least for the purpose of finding geographic and school affinities, Washington is ideal. The only problem with *Martindale* is that it doesn't usually give a person's title, so you can't tell who is an assistant general counsel, deputy assistant general counsel or branch chief. However, either the *Congressional Directory* or the *U.S. Lawyers Reference Directory*, which give the titles of key people and should be used as a supplement to *Martindale*.

Although their scope is limited to the top people, both *Who's Who in Government* and the *Congressional Staff Directory* give biographical information about lawyers which will help you discover other affinities. *Who's Who in Government* will include general counsels and solicitors and perhaps deputy general counsels and deputy solicitors, but it is not likely to include lawyers below that level. The *Congressional Staff Di-*

rectory limits its biographical blurbs to members of Congress, congressional staff members and key members of Senate and House committees, many of whom are lawyers.

Directories of U.S. Attorneys. Although many U.S. Attorneys' offices won't hire anyone who doesn't have a few years experience, there are some U.S. Attorney's offices (all of which are autonomous in their hiring) that do hire people right out of law school or who are very recent graduates. There is no pattern to this, and the only way to find out which offices do hire out of law school and which don't is to write to each one separately. *The National Directory of Law Enforcement Administrators* and the *Register — Department of Justice and United States Courts* both list the names of the U.S. Attorneys and mailing addresses for every office in the country.

Agency Publications
Almost every federal agency that hires lawyers has literature available specifically describing the legal department and the work of attorneys in that agency. Most law school placement offices have abundant supplies of these materials, but if yours does not you can write to any agency and request the literature. There is no central clearinghouse for all the literature of all the agencies. If you write to Washington for materials, you must write to each agency separately. Sometimes the materials prepared by Washington describe the work of the regional offices as well. However, in all cases where you are interested in particular regional offices, you should still contact those offices to see if they prepare their own literature describing attorney positions. Agency publications, often in the form of brochures or pamphlets, should always be read as part of your preparation for an interview.

In addition to the literature that agencies prepare for recruiting purposes, many agencies also publish annual reports which are very detailed accounts of the work of the agency. These provide probably the most detailed and comprehensive information about their work. These will help you prepare for interviews and will be a great aid in helping you decide whether to take a job with an agency that has made you an offer. The National Labor Relations Board, the Civil Aeronautics Board, the Federal Trade Commission and the Pension Guaranty Corporation, for example, all have annual reports that will help you understand the full scope of the work of its lawyers. Annual reports can be obtained from the agencies directly or from the Government Printing Office.

Other Sources

Many of the sources listed in the chapter "Private Firms" are also relevant for federal government job hunting. Even though professional associations, conventions and conferences, continuing education programs and placement services emanate out of and service the private bar, and even though most legal journals (including law reviews) are written by and for private attorneys, these sources should not be completely overlooked by those seeking government positions.

The Federal Bar Association in Washington is a professional association whose membership consists of lawyers who now, or at some time, worked for the government. In addition to running conferences, seminars and lectures, it operates its own placement service which mails a *Placement Service Newsletter* to subscribers each month. Although the Federal Bar Association Placement Service, which solicits job listings in both government and in private firms, was initially geared towards the needs of attorneys with three to five or more years experience, it has recently attempted to become more active regarding recent law graduates.

The faculty for continuing education of the bar workshops often include government attorneys. A program on any of the following subjects will surely include government lawyers; collective bargaining and arbitration (National Labor Relations Board); tax (IRS); anti-trust (Federal Trade Commission and Securities and Exchange Commission); employee benefits or occupational health and safety (Labor); patents (Patent and Trademark Office); energy (Federal Energy Administration); or communications law (Federal Communications Commission).

Newspaper articles also can provide leads. A government lawyer may be mentioned in relation to a case s/he is handling or someone's appointment to a new position may be reported. Perhaps the most useful information newspapers can provide concerns the establishment of new programs as a result of the passage of legislation or for other reasons. In recent years the legal staffs of most agencies have not been increased, and new hiring has primarily been to fill openings created through attrition. However, every now and then new legislation will require additional staffing. When the Pension Reform Act was passed in 1974, the Solicitor's Office of the Department of Labor added a large number of attorneys to its staff. Sometimes new agencies are created by Congress, as was the case of the Federal Election Commission. One recent graduate who read in the newspaper about a new commission created to investigate the problem of federal paperwork was the first person to apply for a position!

Look for government lawyers who have written articles about subjects of interest to you and then contact them. Also, get your hands on alumnae(i) publications, find out which graduates of your college or law school are government attorneys and go visit them.

Whereas it is relatively easy to identify federal agencies that employ lawyers, finding state and local agencies that hire lawyers seems to be problematical for most people. In fact, with the exception of attorneys general's and district attorneys' offices, and the offices of county, city and town attorneys, few other state and local hirers of lawyers come immediately to mind.

State and local government offices simply have less visibility than federal agencies. Since their staff sizes are smaller and there is less attrition, they do much less hiring than federal employers. With the exception of some of the larger attorneys general's, district attorneys' and county attorneys' offices, very few state and local agencies engage in active recruiting. There is also a dearth of literature prepared by non-federal agencies explaining the work of their legal departments. On top of all this, state and local governments have been affected much more than federal agencies by the fiscal problems and budget cutbacks of recent years. As a result, their hiring and visibility have been reduced that much more.

Nevertheless, there are a substantial number of lawyers who work for state and local governments, and opportunities remain for recent law graduates. As a matter of fact, most of the new hiring that occurs is done at the entry level from a pool of relatively inexperienced attorneys.

As a rule of thumb, count on the fact that most major state and local governmental departments will employ at least some lawyers. Although their legal staff size is usually smaller than that of the attorney general, district attorney or county attorney, you can be fairly sure that some lawyers work for the following state and local government departments: labor relations, comptroller, banking, finance, consumer protection, environmental conservation, public utilities, health, education, budget, tax, social services, housing, insurance,

State and Local Government

transportation, economic development, human rights, the legislature, the courts and the offices of the governor, mayor or county executive.

The resources listed for this section direct you to those agencies in different states and localities that are likely to hire lawyers. Some resources will provide you with the name of the top officials within an agency, and some will give you information about the nature of the legal work. However, in most instances you won't readily find this information in publicly available literature. While it is no problem to find the heads of the various divisions of the Department of Justice, finding out who heads the different bureaus of a district attorney's or city attorney's office is often not so easy. Therefore you should look upon the resource listings as starting points only, and be resigned to the fact that you will have to do a lot of writing and calling on your own to find out information about offices, including the best people within them for you to contact.

Also, keep in mind that very few state or local agencies hire much before there is an actual opening to be filled. If you want to work at this level of government, you must be resigned to not getting a job much before, and probably not until after, you graduate. Many attorneys general's and district attorneys' offices will even require that you be admitted to the bar before you are employed.

Finally, a word should be said about the civil service requirements and the political constraints that relate to state and local positions in some places. Although most states and localities exempt attorney positions from civil service competitive examination requirements, some do fill attorney positions from examination lists. New York State and New York City, for example, have both exempt and nonexempt attorney positions. In other places although there might not be civil service requirements, political considerations dictate who gets the available positions. These political considerations can sometimes totally preclude you from ever getting a state or local government position if you lack the entree or connections. No real generalizations can be made about either the civil service or political factors, and each state and locality must be looked at independently.

RESOURCES
State "Blue Books"

Each state publishes its own blue book. (Sometimes, instead of State Blue Book they are called State Manual, State Register, Legislative Manual or Official Directory. New York State publishes a "Red Book"!) These books describe the executive, legislative and judicial branches of the state's government. There usually is a listing of all state agencies, with addresses and phone numbers and the names of the key people within the agency. Sometimes only the very top person will be designated, e.g. the attorney general, or commissioner, or director. However, very often the listing of personnel is quite detailed and will include the chief counsel or general counsel, division or bureau chiefs, and such people as the agency's legislative liaison or labor conciliator.

Usually the description of the attorney general's office, or its equivalent, is comprehensive. The *New Jersey Legislative Manual*, for instance, not only lists the heads of every division within the Department of Law and Public Safety, it lists the names of every lawyer on the staff of each division, indicates when they were hired and states their salary.

Many of the states' blue books will give good descriptions of the work and responsibilities of each agency. Often, biographical information is given for the top officials within each agency. This offers an excellent opportunity to discover affinities with you or people you know based on schools, geographic locations, places of employment, professional associations and clubs.

Several states' blue books include similar information for county, city and town governments within the state. Sometimes municipalities will even publish their own equivalent of a state blue book such as the *New York City Official Directory*, or *Green Book* as it is commonly called.

These blue books are typically published by, and can be purchased from, the secretary of state's office. Most reference sections of libraries, including law libraries, have a collection of blue books. It is probably a good idea for a law school's placement office to have blue books for the state where it is located as well as surrounding states and anywhere else its students seem to be especially interested in. *State Blue Books and Reference Publications* or the *Guide to American Directories* contain bibliographies of the available blue books.

Beyond what has already been said, there are not many other generalizations that can be made about different states' blue books. Some contain much more information than others, but in all cases you should consult them. You will be surprised at the tidbits of information you can pick up. You might discover that the starting salary for a recent graduate, upon admission to the bar, in the Alaska Attorney General's Office is about $25,000!

Other Directories

Although none of the sources listed under this heading are as detailed as the blue books, often they will be more accessible to you. At most, they give you the name of the agency and perhaps the name of the top person (though usually not the top legal officer) so use them only as starting points — for names and addresses where you can get additional information.

The National Directory of State Agencies lists the major agencies for every state. There is a state-by-state listing as well as a listing according to function. The name, address and top official is given for each agency. Although a state's environmental affairs department may have a huge legal staff headed by a chief counsel and various bureau chiefs, this directory will give only the name of the agency's commissioner, director or chief.

Who's Who in Government will have biographical information only about the very top people in state, county and city government. Also, it is not published every year, so many top officials are not included, and several who are no longer hold office. However, you should make whatever use of it you can, and for some of the larger states and localities it can be quite helpful.

Sometimes just going through a phone book under state, county, city or town government will give you a good overview of the scope and structure of a governmental organization. It is easy to go down the list of agencies in a phone directory and pinpoint those that are likely to have a legal staff. Since offices with the same function are often called by different names in different places, this is a good way to familiarize yourself with the terminology used in other states or localities.

Always check to see what information a state or local government offers. A state personnel office or civil service commission might prepare literature. New Jersey, at least in the recent past, has prepared a list of its agencies that hired attorneys. Or, by visiting state or county office buildings, see if you can get a hold of a phone directory which, as they did for federal agencies, will give the organizational breakdown of an office and the names of staff people within it.

Publications for Attorneys General and District Attorneys

Although most of the sources already listed will give the name and address of attorneys general, an additional source is *The National Directory of Law Enforcement Administrators*. This book, which also is a national listing of district attorneys or county prosecutors, does not give very precise mailing addresses, however. Addressing a letter to "Office of Attorney General," "State Department of law," "Office of District Attorney," or "County Prosecutor's Office" in the appropriate state or county office building will usually be sufficient. At least as regards district attorneys or county prosecutors, *The National Directory of Prosecuting Attorneys* is a comprehensive listing, including detailed and accurate mailing addresses.

Many attorneys general and district attorneys offices, especially those that do active recruiting, publish their own materials that describe the structure and work of their office. Also, annual reports are usually excellent resources.

A really first-rate source of information is the National Association of Attorneys General. Its Committee on the Office of Attorney General, for example, periodically publishes a report entitled *Selected Statistics on the Office of Attorney General*. This report gives an organizational breakdown of the attorney general's office of each state, indicates the total number of lawyers employed, shows the distribution of lawyers among the various divisions and even gives salary information for all offices. Even though figures might not be absolutely current, they do give you a sense of the size of different offices and the distribution of staff within them. You will discover that the attorney general's office for the state of Oregon employs just over 100 attorneys, Rhode Island about 30 and Montana only about ten. On the other hand, California's office of the attorney general employs over 400 lawyers, and New York's over 500.

You can see that in the attorney general's office in

Vermont there are only a couple of attorney positions in the environmental division. Ohio's environmental law section employs about 20 attorneys. If your interests are well defined, this kind of a distribution breakdown will point you to those offices that have large staffs in your area of interests. The size of different bureau staffs will indicate where the most opportunities seem to lie, and thereby can aid you in deciding what interests of yours you should pursue.

For several states, this report also gives information regarding lawyers employed by state agencies, boards and commissions other than the attorney general's office — the total number and the distribution between the different agencies. South Carolina has only about 30 attorneys employed by the state outside its attorney general's office. Pennsylvania employs over 400. And within the state of Pennsylvania, although only about ten attorneys work in the Department of Education, about 70 are employed by the Department of Transportation. This report, then, is an excellent guide for establishing initial impressions about where legal opportunities within state government seem to be — what states and what agencies within a state.

Newspapers

Articles constantly report news relating to state and local agencies. The cases involving attorneys general's and district attorneys' offices make the news daily. The cases of other agencies, and the particular attorneys handling them, are also reported — typically for the following departments: consumer protection, environmental affairs, public utilities, workmen's compensation, mediation and arbitration, human rights, housing and development, corporation counsel or city attorney.

Following an election there will invariably be news about new appointees, including a vast number of lawyers. In fact, if you are interested in a government position out of state, go through back issues of papers of a particular state or locality.

Martindale-Hubbell
Martindale, of course, is always useful. Especially for smaller localities, it will help you identify (by going through the front section under a specific geographic area) those offices that employ lawyers. You will also get a sense of the staff size of an agency. It is easy to see how many times the office of the county attorney, for example, comes up under one geographic listing.

Public 7
Interest

"From the beginning, the public interest lawyers became an establishment bar of a different sort, made up of the brightest graduates of the best law schools, the editors of the law reviews, the law clerks to Supreme Court justices, the disillusioned refugees from the more prestigious corporate firms."

From an article about public
interest law in The New York Times,
July, 1975

"I have never known anyone who really wanted a public interest job who has not gotten one."

An attorney for a Washington, D.C.
public interest law center

Public interest law means different things to different people. Here it is defined as giving legal services to clients and for causes that have historically been unrepresented or under-represented by the legal community. It includes places that provide individual representation to clients who are indigent or members of minorities.

And it includes programs that are primarily concerned with broad issues and law reform — rather than individual client representation — in such areas as civil rights, women's rights, environmental protection, health (including mental health), consumer protection, tax reform, prison reform, corporate responsibility, housing, education and workers' rights. With the exception of the government-funded legal services programs and public defenders' offices, public interest law firms and programs in this chapter primarily are nongovernmental.

Since different work-settings for public interest law present unique opportunities and problems, this chapter has been organized according to the various settings, and separate observations have been made about each one.

LEGAL SERVICES PROGRAMS

These are programs that are federally funded by the Legal Services Corporation to provide free legal services to poor people in civil cases. Legal services, or poverty law offices, are now established in every state as well as the District of Columbia, Puerto Rico, Micronesia and the Virgin Islands. Offices have been organized on a state, county or city basis, and there are presently about 300 separate programs that employ around 3,000 lawyers.

Legal services programs provide some of the best public interest law opportunities for recent graduates. Apart from their size and pervasiveness throughout the country, compared to most other public interest programs, they are stably funded. In fact, the funding level for the Legal Services Corporation seems to be expanding and new programs are being created. Increased funding has meant more hiring and higher salaries.

Poverty law offices are fairly receptive to hiring recent law graduates. Because of the many opportunities law students have to work in poverty law offices — through their school's clinical programs or during the summer (especially through federal work-study) — they can become much more experienced in poverty law than many other areas of the law. Also, since many states permit law graduates who work for legal services offices limited rights to practice (often including courtroom representation) while awaiting the results of the bar exam, or full rights to practice if you're admitted in another state, it is not as imperative as in other public interest offices that you be admitted to the bar of the state where the program is located. You can contribute a substantial amount to a legal services program prior to admission, whereas your contribution might be minimal to a public interest law firm that is not covered by special practice rules.

In addition to regular staff attorney positions that become available through increased funding ar attrition, the Reginald Heber Smith Community Lawyer Fellowship Program ("Reggie Program") and VISTA offer alternative routes to legal services offices. The "Reggie Program" provides about 125 new fellowships each year for recent graduates to work in legal services programs. These are one-year fellowships that can be renewed for a second year, and in limited cases can even be extended for a third year.

VISTA also places lawyers in poverty law offices, and although the compensation is a subsistence level stipend (compared to the "Reggie" salary that is close to the starting salaries of legal services staff attorneys), it offers an excellent "foot in the door" to legal services. It is also a good way to assume control over what program you work for. Since VISTA lawyers constitute the pool from which new staff attorneys are chosen for many offices, it is often the only way for an inexperienced attorney to get on the staff of certain of the most sought after offices, i.e. those on either coast.

Legal services jobs are relatively plentiful only when compared to other public interest law positions. In the context of the total job market, the opportunities are still somewhat limited. Therefore it is usually necessary that people have prior exposure to poverty law, e.g. through clinical experience, in order to be considered a strong candidate for a position with most legal services offices.

The greatest frustration for law students who seek jobs in poverty law offices is the inability to secure a position before graduation. With very few exceptions (the "Reggie" fellowships, for instance, are given out around March of each year), legal services programs simply don't hire in advance, and you have to resign yourself to that fact. This does not mean you should not contact programs during the early part of your third year. Just don't expect a job offer then. But do interview with different programs, find out which are the best offices, and discuss the possibility of working as a "Reggie" or VISTA attorney as well as a staff attorney. Lay the groundwork so that later you will be following up rather than making initial contact.

STATE AND LOCALLY FUNDED LEGAL AID (CIVIL AND CRIMINAL)
Although most of the representation of poor people in civil matters is now done through the federal legal services programs, there still are a few non-federal, publicly funded civil programs that exist in lieu of, or in addition to them. Often called "legal aid" or "legal aid-civil" (though many of the federal legal services have "legal aid" in their title as well), these offices are typically very small and offer relatively few opportunities

for jobs compared to legal services programs. Therefore, what is said under this heading pertains primarily to state and locally funded *criminal* defense programs. (With the exception of federal public defenders' offices, which are fairly small, are limited to large cities where federal courts are located, and rarely hire inexperienced lawyers, there is no federal analog to the Legal Services Corporation in the criminal law area.)

Criminal defenders' or public defenders' offices (sometimes also called "legal aid" or "legal aid-criminal") represent indigent clients in criminal cases, at both the trial and appellate level. They are located in all states and often have large staff sizes. The New York City Legal Aid Society-Criminal Division, for example, employs over 500 attorneys. Although many of these programs have felt the effects of state and local government fiscal problems, they still are much more financially secure than most privately funded or foundation-supported public interest law programs.

Criminal defenders' offices, like legal services programs, tend to be receptive to hiring recent graduates. Law students' experiences often include criminal clinical programs, trial practice and other activities that would make you more than absolutely green in a criminal defense office. Also, many defenders' offices benefit from the same special practice rules as programs that represent indigent clients in civil matters.

Perhaps criminal defenders' offices offer the most opportunities of any public interest employer because of the very high turnover rate that has traditionally characterized these programs. Although this has been reduced in many instances by raising salaries and by the limits the tight job market has placed on mobility, these offices still have fairly constant turnover, and, therefore, openings. Nevertheless, only the very largest offices will attempt to predict their turnover and hire in advance of the time an opening actually occurs.

FOUNDATION SUPPORTED PUBLIC INTEREST LAW FIRMS	Unlike legal services programs or criminal defenders offices whose attorneys handle individual service caseloads, public interest law firms take on high impact, policy-making matters and law reform and test case litigation. These are mostly foundation-supported programs. However, the Legal Services Corporation specialized litigation and support centers have also been included since they handle the same types of cases, and the job opportunity problems that relate to foundation-supported public interest law firms apply to them as well.

Public interest law firms characteristically have small staffs with little turnover; fill positions with lawyers who have had substantial experience in a relevant field; are highly sought after places to work and are geographically bunched in the Northeast and California. The effect of all this is that opportunities, especially for recent graduates, are limited — certainly as compared to legal services and criminal defenders programs.

Nevertheless, public interest firms should not be written off completely as possible places to work after graduating from law school. Just remember, it is highly unlikely for you to receive serious consideration without a substantial amount of prior exposure and experience in the precise area of concern to an office, and, ideally, you should have worked for that very program on a part-time or summer basis throughout law school. The Natural Resources Defense Council (New York City, Washington, D.C. and Palo Alto, California), Legal Action Center (New York City), Center for Law and Social Policy (Washington, D.C.), Children's Defense Fund (Washington, D.C., New York City, Cambridge, Massachusetts, Austin, Texas, and Jackson, Mississippi), National Health Law Program (Los Angeles), Public Advocates (San Francisco), Connecticut Women's Educational and Legal Fund (New Haven, Connecticut) or Indiana Center on Law and Poverty (Indianapolis) to name but a few of the public interest law firms, simply would not hire you right out of law school unless you had worked for them or a related program and had proved yourself unusually competent and experienced. In other words, you must evolve into a position as opposed to making initial contact sometime during your third year of law school or shortly after you graduate.

You must make your commitment to public interest law during law school. Volunteer, get on federal work-study, work for "peanuts" and apply for what few paying internships exist. Whether you're looking during or after law school, remember that the field of public interest law is relatively small, especially within specific geographic areas or particular substantive fields. Therefore, it is very easy to find out who's doing what, where. If you find one person doing prison reform litigation in the Southwest, s/he will tell you everyone else in that part of the country doing the same and will know most of the attorneys involved with prison reform in other parts of the country as well. And chances are good that s/he will know of lawyers in other public interest fields both in that part of the country and elsewhere. There are just not that many people doing health law, or education law, or senior citizens law or even environmental law. In fact, the public interest law grapevine is probably the easiest of all to plug into. But don't just inquire about a job opening — ask for advice and names of people to contact.

No matter what your credentials are, don't ever expect to be offered a position with a public interest law firm much before you are actually able to begin work. Staff sizes are too small and funding situations are too unpredictable to allow these programs to hire before an opening exists and you are ready to fill it.

CIVIL RIGHTS AND CIVIL LIBERTIES CENTERS

The problems already discussed become exacerbated in regard to those offices that specifically litigate civil rights and civil liberties issues. These centers also have small staffs and few openings that are not replaced with highly experienced litigators. But in addition they loom as the most visible and most desirable of all places to work for the public interest-minded graduate. Few law students and law graduates have not heard of the ACLU, NAACP Legal Defense and Education Fund, the Southern Poverty Law Center, the Lawyers' Committee for Civil Rights Under Law or the Center for Constitutional Rights.

Absent some extraordinary credential, e.g. Editor-in-Chief of the Yale Law Journal, you cannot send off a resume to the national office of the American Civil Liberties Union during your third year and expect to get hired as a staff attorney — or even to get interviewed. You must have established a long, on-going relationship with a program during law school to expect a staff position when you graduate. This does not simply mean working for one summer or spending one semester as an intern. It's a long-term contact during which substantial work is done, much experience is obtained, and superior ability and competence are demonstrated. A woman who worked for the New York Civil Liberties Union in an administrative capacity for a couple of years before going to law school, continued working there throughout each school year and summer, and then was offered a staff position upon graduating from law school — the result of a five-or six-year association. This is the kind of scenario that is necessary if you wish to get a job with one of these most attractive of public interest law programs at the time you graduate from law school.

Although there are several varieties of group legal services plans, this discussion relates primarily to those pre-paid plans sponsored by labor unions, since they presently are the largest and most organized, and have staffs of full-time attorneys as opposed to a panel of participating lawyers. Union members' dues contributions entitle them to legal services coverage in much the same way that other dues contributions entitle them to health, disability or pension benefits.

GROUP LEGAL SERVICES PROGRAMS (AND LABOR UNIONS)

The pre-paid group legal services movement is definitely on the rise and will hopefully create many public interest law opportunities in the future. Presently, only a few unions have large full-time legal staffs. The Municipal Employees Legal Services Fund sponsored by District Council 37 of the American Federation of State and County Municipal Employees in New York City now employs a staff of full-time lawyers that numbers about 30. The legal matters handled by this and similar plans correspond pretty much with the kinds of cases handled by federally funded legal services programs. They are civil matters, primarily in the areas of domestic relations, housing (landlord-tenant), consumer affairs, contracts and wills.

Because of their similarity to legal services, or poverty law offices, pre-paid group legal services plans offer the same kind of opportunity to recent graduates. The major limitation on the number of opportunities is the fact that only a few plans of substantial legal staff size presently exist. But since this number is now growing, keep close tabs on where new plans are being created and old plans are being expanded.

Aside from the group legal plans unions now sponsor, unions offer many other opportunities for public interest legal work. All unions employ legal counsel, either in-house or on retainer. Some unions have large legal departments, and opportunities for lawyers exist there as well as in other union departments such as those related to legislative affairs, government relations and health and pension funds. Recent graduates who have established solid labor law credentials through both course work and work experience often can realistically compete for union legal positions.

ATTORNEYS IN PRIVATE PRACTICE

Lawyers in private practice are involved with public interest law in a variety of settings. Private firms do public interest work with varying degrees of time and resource commitment. At one extreme are the law firms, including law communes or collectives, that handle little else besides public interest matters. At the other extreme are the large corporate firms that allow associates and partners to devote some amount of their time to non-fee-producing public interest cases. In between are all sorts of hybrids. There are some small firms which in addition to a general practice devote substantial — maybe even half — time to public interest cases. There is even one large Washington, D.C. corporate firm that has a "Pro Bono Department" which is headed by a partner who devotes full time to handling public interest cases. He is assisted by some other partners and by several associates who "rotate" through the pro bono department just as they go through the tax, litigation or corporate departments.

In addition to firms, there are a number of other mechanisms through which attorneys in private practice work on public interest concerns. Several bar associations (i.e. Beverly Hills and Boston) sponsor offices that do public interest law, and bar association members volunteer to assist in the handling of cases. Some bar associations, instead of creating, funding and staffing an office, simply maintain a panel of attorneys who donate their time to public interest matters.

The Council of New York Law Associates, the Chicago Council of Lawyers and the Washington, D.C. Council of Lawyers are among the programs that are funded through some combination of contributions from private firms and foundations that provide legal help for public interest cases from its membership rolls of private attorneys. In New York City private firms contribute to the maintenance of the Community Law Office located in Harlem which uses private attorneys to volunteer in the servicing of the poor of that community.

Although in most localities there exists some mechanism through which the private bar engages in public interest law, the involvement is more often than not on a volunteer and very part-time basis. The full-time, paying opportunities to work for a private law firm and to do mostly public interest law are very limited. However, because of their limitedness, what few places exist are easy enough to find.

Although they will not be repeated here, many of the sources listed in prior chapters, e.g. professional associations, conferences and conventions, continuing education of the bar programs, newspaper articles and alumnae(i) directories certainly are useful in looking for public interest law jobs as well.

The resources here are organized according to public interest work setting. There will, however, be lots of overlap in the sense that something listed for one kind of place will also offer information about others. There-

RESOURCES

fore, although sources are identified with the setting for which they primarily apply, anyone interested in any public interest law type of work should become familiar with the materials listed under all headings.

General Aids

Information Resources For Public Interest. This is a very comprehensive listing of people, places and publications devoted to public interest concerns, including public interest law. Don't be put off by the fact that it looks like a computer printout. It is worth figuring out how this directory is organized and how to use it. It will be tremendously useful for identifying people and programs all around the country.

Human Rights Organizations and Periodicals Directory. This directory is published by the Meiklejohn Civil Liberties Institute. The Institute distributes a vast collection of publications relating to human rights. The *Directory* is "intended as a referral list for people seeking information or assistance in human rights cases." Groups, programs and publications are listed alphabetically as well as under subject matter. The following subject headings give an idea of the wide scope of this directory: civil liberties; discrimination based on age, national origin, race, religion or sex (also listings under blacks, Asians, chicanos, native Americans and women); consumer protection; education; labor/employment; health (mental patients); farmworkers; migrants; aliens; homosexuals; housing; poverty/welfare; prisoners; youth; unions; and repression.

Encyclopedia of Associations. The *Encyclopedia* gives the name, address, phone number and executive director for each program it lists. In addition it gives some indication of the staff size of each office as well as a description of the work it does. Most of the public interest law programs can be found under the headings "Legal Organizations," "Social Welfare Organizations," or "Public Affairs Organizations."

Under "Legal Organizations" you'll find such places as the Center on Social Welfare Policy and Law (New York City), Environmental Law Institute (Washington, D.C), Mexican American Legal Defense and Educational Fund (San Francisco), National Consumer Law Center (Boston) and the Western Center on Law and Poverty (Los Angeles). "Social Welfare Organizations" include Legal Services for the Elderly Poor (New York City), Society for Animal Rights (New York City), Food Research and Action Center (Washington, D.C.), and the National Employment Law Project (New York City).

Most of the civil rights and civil liberties centers are listed under "Public Affairs Organizations." These would include the ACLU, Center for Constitutional Rights, National Emergency Civil Liberties Committee, Anti-Defamation League of B'nai Brith, NAACP Legal Defense and Education Fund and the Southern Poverty Law Center.

Harvard Law School Public Interest Questionnaire. Each year the Placement Office of Harvard Law School surveys public interest employers throughout the United States. The results of this survey can be subscribed to by other law school placement offices. Although most of the responses come from legal services and criminal defenders' programs, there are a number of listings from the entire spectrum of public interest law employers. This is a particularly good source for finding private attorneys and firms that do public interest law.

The questionnaires give the name(s) of the attorney(s) responsible for doing the hiring for each program and indicate anticipated openings for experienced attorneys, June graduates and summer interns. No other single source collects this kind of information, and for this reason the *Harvard Questionnaire* is invaluable.

Law Students Civil Rights Research Council Report. LSCRRC publishes a report on their summer law student internship programs which lists public interest law offices where interns have worked. It is a good overview of many of the most active public interest employers, including a description of the kind of cases that an office handles. This report is also an excellent way of discovering many of the private lawyers and law firms that litigate civil rights and other public interest cases.

Alternatives. This is a newsletter published by the American Bar Association Consortium on Legal Services and the Public. It reports news relating to public interest law, announces conferences, publicizes new books and other publications and even lists positions available in various public interest law settings. Names of public interest lawyers as well as specific programs are mentioned in abundance, making this a good source to browse through for leads.

Legal Services Programs

Clearinghouse Review. This is an essential resource for anyone interested in poverty law. Although this monthly publication has a substantial "Positions Available in Legal Services" section, announcing immediate openings, this section is useful only if you've already graduated from law school and are available to begin work. The real utility of this periodical, however, is in regard to the other information it provides — articles about various issues in poverty law, cases that have been or presently are being litigated, and books and journals in various subject areas.

Going through cases reported in several back issues

of the *Clearinghouse* will give you an excellent idea as to major individuals and programs in a particular field of poverty law. If, for example, you went through a year's back issues under the heading of "education law," you would see certain lawyers and programs often identified with the education law cases that were reported. If education law was the area of special interest to you, this would be the best way of finding the most obvious places to which to apply or, at least, to contact for information and additional leads. You could do this for any of the subject areas under which cases are reported, including the following substantive fields in poverty law: consumer, domestic relations, employment, food, health, housing, immigration, Indian, juvenile, mental health, migrant, prison, social security, unemployment compensation and welfare.

Also, reading the summaries of cases reported in particular fields of poverty law is probably the best way to prepare for a job interview with a legal services program.

National Legal Aid and Defender Association Publications. NLADA, a professional association for lawyers who represent indigent clients in both civil and criminal cases, publishes a newsletter, *Washington Memo,* as well as a periodical, *Briefcase.* Both these publications report current developments relating to poverty law. The *Washington Memo* also includes the "NLADA Placement Service" which lists immediate job openings in offices all over the country.

In addition, NLADA publishes a *Directory of Legal Aid and Defender Offices* which includes a national listing of federally funded legal services programs as well as state or locally funded legal aid–civil offices. (This listing is also reproduced in Volume VI of *Martindale-Hubbell.*)

Legal Services Corporation Program Directory. Since this directory is always being updated, it is the best listing of federally funded legal services programs. Also, since it gives the name of the director of each program, it is a more useful directory than the one published by the National Legal Aid and Defender Association which does not offer that information. Remember, it is always preferable to direct applications and inquiries to a person within an office rather than to merely the office address itself.

DOMESTIC PROGRAMS

ACTION Fact Book. For those people interested in working for a legal services program as a VISTA attorney, this could serve as a very useful resource. Published every six months, it lists all programs around the country that have sponsored VISTA volunteers. It enables you to identify those programs that have received VISTA lawyers in the past, and therefore are likely to receive them in the future. It also indicates the number of volunteers a program sponsors, information that might help you decide which are the more likely offices to be interested in taking you on as a VISTA attorney.

Since programs that have been designated to receive VISTA lawyers can request the specific people they want, the VISTA route is an excellent way to both control where you will work and to get a commitment before you graduate from law school.

Publications of Specific Legal Services Programs. Aside from the *Legal ,Services Corporation News* which is published by the Legal Services Corporation in Washington, D.C., many of the individual programs publish their own newsletters reporting their activities and announcing positions that are available. If you are interested in a particular office, it would be a good idea to find out if it puts out its own publication. The larger programs are more likely to do so. Community Action for Legal Services, for example, which is the legal services program for New York City, publishes a bimonthly newsletter entitled *The Law & The Poor*.

National Legal Aid and Defender Association Publications. In addition to lawyers who work for federal legal services offices, NLADA's membership consists of lawyers in non-federal legal aid-civil programs. It also consists of criminal defenders, including federal public defenders. Therefore, its publications are good sources of information about these programs. The *Directory* is especially useful for its listing of criminal defenders' or public defenders' offices.

State and Locally Funded Legal Aid (Civil and Criminal)

    Poverty Law Reporter. The "Office-Project Locator" section of this reporter, published by the Commerce Clearing House, lists all civil and criminal programs that represent poor clients. Although some of the information is often not current, the Locator section is a good starting point if some of the better sources already mentioned are not available.

Balancing the Scales of Justice: Financing Public Interest Law in America. This report was prepared by the Council for Public Interest Law in Washington, D.C. In the context of this report about the problems of financing public interest law programs, there is an excellent and comprehensive survey of approximately 90 public interest law firms, including the specialized litigation and support centers funded by the Legal Services Corporation.

Foundation-Supported Public Interest Law Firms

    Balancing the Scales of Justice includes a directory of public interest law centers, organized by state, which summarizes the kind of work each center does and also gives information about the staff size of each program. For these reasons, it is clearly the single best source for discovering the major public interest law offices and for learning the scope of public interest law activities.

This report also offers a very good analysis of the background and evolution of the public interest law movement. Two other good sources for background reading are *Public Interest Law: Five Years Later*, prepared by the Ford Foundation and the American Bar Association, and "Lawyers for Social Change: Perspectives on Public Interest Law," published in Volume 28 of the *Stanford Law Review*. Both these studies cite and describe the work of numerous public interest programs.

Martindale-Hubbell. Volume VI of *Martindale* includes a section on "Public Interest Practice Firms and Organizations." Under this heading is a state-by-state listing of tax-exempt public interest law firms and organizations (does not include private law firms which do public interest work). With each listing there is a descriptive blurb about the general area of concern of that office, e.g. consumer affairs, health and mental health problems, foreign affairs, environment, women's rights and prisoners' rights.

Jobs in Social Change. This book surveys public interest groups in Washington, D.C. One chapter is devoted to "Public Interest Law" specifically, while other chapters include "Human Rights and Civil Liberties," "Children's Rights," "Consumer Protection," "Environment," "Health," "Prison Reform," and "Women." For each program there is information about its work, which includes a listing of current cases or projects, as well as information about its staff size and funding level. Although this book is based on information compiled in 1975, it is still very revealing and should certainly be used by anyone who has a specific interest in working in Washington.

The Foundation Grants Index. Since almost all public interest law firms receive at least some foundation support (even federal legal services specialized litigation and support centers often get foundation monies to support particular projects), going through back issues of *The Foundation Grants Index* will point you to most of the existing public interest programs. The subject index provides an easy way to find programs in particular areas. Look under the following headings: "Law," "Legal Aid," "Legal Defense," "Environment," "Civil Rights," "Minorities," "Mental Health" or any other subject area of interest to you.

Not only is the *Grants Index* a good way to discover the existence of certain programs, it is a useful device for discovering which programs have recently received funding and in what amount. Since new grants often coincide with new staffing needs, this provides a good mechanism for finding those centers that have both the need and the money to hire. Also, since grants are described according to their purpose, the *Grants Index* could lead you to projects that very precisely relate to your interests and experience.

Conservation Directory and *Directory of Environmental Groups.* The *Conservation Directory*, prepared by the National Wildlife Federation, and the *Directory of Environmental Groups*, prepared on a regional basis by that region's office of the U.S. Environmental Protection Agency, are comprehensive listings of environmental groups — governmental and non-governmental, legal and non-legal.

Newsletters and Publications of Specific Programs. Almost every public interest law center puts out materials that describe its activities as well as those of other groups working in the same area of the law. Some examples of these types of publications include: *Pipeline* (Council for Public Interest Law); *Health Law Newsletter* (National Health Law Program); *Public Citizen Report* (various Nader groups); *Annual Report* (Center for Law and Health Sciences); and *Docket of Cases* (Natural Resources Defense Council).

The scope of information that you find in these publications is far-reaching. For example, the *Docket* prepared by the Natural Resources Defense Council includes a listing of attorneys in private practice who worked on NRDC cases on a pro bono basis. This listing, together with those people listed on NRDC's Board of Trustees, gives you an extensive pool of lawyers that could be useful sources of information about environmental law opportunities.

Specialized Journals. Journals that are organized around a field of public interest law include articles written by lawyers who practice in that field. Therefore, these journals serve as a useful tool for identifying attorneys and programs in areas of public interest law of interest to you. *The Ecology Law Quarterly, Columbia Journal of Environmental Law, Columbia Journal of Law & Social Problems*, the *Bulletin of the American Academy of Psychiatry and the Law* or the *American Indian Law Review* are examples of this type of publication.

Civil Rights and Civil Liberties Centers

Several of the sources previously listed are also useful for locating those places that specifically are concerned with civil rights matters, so refer back to them. The *Human Rights Organizations and Periodicals Directory* is certainly a primary resource. Among other things it lists every regional and affiliate office of the American Civil Liberties Union. *Balancing the Scales of Justice* and the *Foundation Grants Index* should also be consulted. Below are some additional sources.

Civil Rights Directory. This directory, published by the U.S. Commission on Civil Rights, lists nongovernmental civil rights organizations in addition to its list of federal agencies that have civil rights responsibilities. The organizations in this directory include those that have legal staffs and do litigation as well as those that have no legal staff as such and engage in research and educational activities primarily.

Newsletters of Programs and Specialized Journals. Civil rights centers, as do most public interest law programs, prepare publications to keep people within the civil rights community abreast of their activities. The Lawyers' Committee for Civil Rights Under Law's *Committee Report* is typical of this kind of publication. Along with reporting on major cases, it reports news of activities, people and events of interest to lawyers who litigate civil rights issues.

Articles in journals will give you leads to civil rights attorneys. *The Civil Liberties Review* (sponsored by the ACLU), the *Columbia Human Rights Law Review* and the *Harvard Civil Rights-Civil Liberties Review* are among the most important of these journals.

National Consumer Center for Legal Services. In addition to providing information and technical assistance for the development of group legal services programs, this center distributes a wealth of materials about group legal services plans, particularly pre-paid plans. Its newsletter, *Group Legal Review*, reports new developments and is an excellent source for discovering new, or newly planned programs. Also, from the Center you can

Group Legal Services Programs (and Labor Unions)

obtain the publication *Early Experience With Group Legal Services*. This case history of the group plan set-up by the Washington, D.C. Laborers' District Council of the Laborers' International Union provides useful background information about pre-paid plans.

Group Legal Services. This is a report prepared by Cornell University's School of Industrial and Labor Relations. Aside from giving excellent background information about the evolution of group legal services programs, it surveys some of the major group plans now in operation in the United States.

Directories of Unions. The best listing of unions is the *Directory of National Unions and Employee Associations*, published by the U.S. Department of Labor, Bureau of Labor Statistics. It gives the names of the key officials in each union, including the heads of the legal department and law related offices, e.g. legislative affairs. *National Trade and Professional Associations of the United States and Canada and Labor Unions* is also a good listing of nationally based unions. *Directory of Public Employee Organizations* is useful though it limits its listing to those unions that represent state and local public employees.

There are also a number of publications that list only the unions of a particular state or locality. State labor departments usually prepare these directories. *The Commonwealth of Massachusetts Directory of Labor Organizations* and the *Directory of Employee Organizations in New York State* are two such examples. On the local level the New York City Central Labor Council AFL-CIO, for example, publishes the *Trade Union Handbook* which lists international and local unions located in New York City. Alternatively, telephone directory yellow pages will list unions under "labor organizations."

Since attorneys in private practice are involved in all facets of public interest law and contribute their services through a variety of settings, all resources listed under the previous headings in this chapter should be considered as sources of information about these lawyers. In addition, the following resources should prove to be especially useful. **Attorneys in Private Practice**

National Lawyers Guild Publications. The National Lawyers Guild is an organization of lawyers and legal workers devoted to giving legal assistance to the movement for social change in the United States. Its publications will lead you to lawyers involved in þublic interest law, many of whom are in private practice (though a substantial number of Guild members work for criminal defenders' offices, legal services and foundation-supported programs). These lawyers will, in turn, lead you to still others. Both its national publications such as *Guild Notes* and regional publications like *Blind Justice* (New York City Chapter) print articles of legal and political significance written by members who are usually identified with the place where they work. Its journal, *Guild Practitioner*, is also a good source of leads to lawyers and programs.

Directories of Guild members can be very useful. The New York City Chapter has published a *Lawyers Referral Directory* which lists members who are in private practice in New York City, Southern Connecticut and Northern New Jersey. This directory even breaks down practices into particular fields such as consumer law, juvenile, welfare, civil rights and liberties, criminal, immigration, labor, employment discrimination, unemployment, workmen's compensation, military, prison, and housing, to name just some of the substantive areas. For this reason the *Directory* is an invaluable resource for finding lawyers in areas of the law you specifically wish to pursue.

Also, the Guild is organized on both a national and regional basis into various committees and projects around particular problems, e.g. labor, immigration, grand juries, prisons, racism or housing. These committees provide an alternative route for finding lawyers interested and involved in particular fields of public interest law.

Publications of Volunteer Programs. Many bar association and foundation supported programs that use the voluntary services of private attorneys publish newsletters that will identify who they are and what cases or projects they are working on. The Council of New York Law Associates' *Newsletter* (or similar publications for Councils in other cities, i.e. Washington and Chicago) is useful, especially if you use your imagination. The roster of teams in the basketball league the Council sponsors can even give you the names of private attorneys who presumably have some involvement in public interest law!

There are certain programs that provide specialized kinds of legal assistance through the voluntary efforts of lawyers in private practice. These groups also usually publish literature. Volunteer Lawyers for the Arts and their publication, *Art and the Law*, is a good example.

Corporations 8

"Signs are better for lawyers wanting positions as in-house counsel. There seems to be a trend in some corporations toward either enlarging or improving legal staffs — and the salaries that go with the jobs."

Juris Doctor, February, 1974

"Studies conducted by the Lawyer Placement Information Service [of the ABA] indicate that roughly only one corporation in every ten presently employs in-house counsel."

Where Do I Go From Here?
by Frances Utley — 1973

Law students and graduates probably know less about job opportunities in corporate legal departments than in any other law setting — certainly as compared to private law firms and government agencies. Corporations have simply not been very visible as potential employers of recent law graduates. Compared to other legal employers, corporations do little on-campus recruiting, literature about corporate legal departments is not widespread, and the corporate in-house lawyer, as a model, is not well known.

133

Compounding the problem of lack of visibility is the assumption that corporate legal departments only hire people with a few years' experience. Although this was true of corporations years ago, and is still more characteristic of corporations than of private firms or government employers, there certainly have been major reversals to this trend. Today, as the size of corporate legal departments has grown, there has been a willingness on the part of many corporations to hire people right out of law school. Unfortunately, many others continue to perpetuate the myth that corporations hire only experienced attorneys, and law school placement offices, law students and law graduates have too readily accepted this. Countless times, a placement director at one law school will be told by corporations that they didn't hire anyone without a couple of years experience, only to find those same corporations scheduled to interview third-year students at Harvard, Yale or Columbia!

The smaller legal departments, or those that do very specialized kinds of work, will, for the most part, seek attorneys who have practiced with a firm for a few years. Very often an associate with a large corporate law firm who has worked on matters concerning a particular corporate client will ultimately go to work for that client. Corporations that employ only an attorney or two in-house usually cannot hire a lawyer who does not have some solid experience related to the legal work required by the corporation. However, many of the corporations with large legal departments (they can number over 100 attorneys) can — and do — hire graduates without any experience. Also, many of those departments that claim to look for experienced attorneys will accept someone with fairly limited experience, say a year. So, be careful about the "experienced only" epithet. Total acceptance of it by the inexperienced law graduate will make it a self-fulfilling prophecy.

You should have an awareness of those corporations that are likely to have a large legal department, since they are the ones most likely to hire recent graduates. The size of the law department is not necessarily a function of the size of the corporation itself. Some of the largest corporations employ only a few attorneys in-house and, instead, retain a large corporate law firm to handle its legal affairs. The size of an in-house legal department is more a function of the kind of legal problems a corporation is likely to have on an on-going basis. Companies that have lots of claims, patent, copyright, tax, government contracts, securities and anti-trust problems usually have a sizeable legal staff.

The following types of companies often employ a substantial number of lawyers: insurance companies; banks; trust companies; brokerage, investment and other financial institutions; title companies; public utilities (telephone companies and power companies); airlines; realty companies; entertainment industry companies (television and film companies, publishers, talent agencies and ad agencies); trade associations and some large retail chains. Also, because of their many patent problems, the following industries have large in-house legal departments: oil and gas companies; chemical, food and pharmaceutical companies; electronics firms and metal manufacturers.

From the above list of corporations with large law departments, the employers that seem particularly receptive to hiring recent graduates include the insurance companies, banks and trust companies, title companies, public utilities and those companies that employ patent attorneys (insofar as recent graduates have the requisite engineering, chemical, electronics or general scientific background).

Since law students and law graduates often become stymied in their attempts to compile lists of corporate legal departments, the resources section of this chapter will be devoted to overcoming that impasse. Also, the resources will help you discover the appropriate person to contact. It is almost always a mistake to send a resume to a personnel office of a corporation. Legal departments do their own hiring, so don't deal with personnel offices despite the oft-repeated injunctions to do so.

At a minimum, direct applications and inquiries to the general counsel — preferably by name. However, since the general counsel is usually also an officer of the company and not necessarily integral to the hiring process at its initial stages, very often it is best to contact an assistant general counsel, senior counsel, or senior tax counsel, for example, who has direct responsibility for screening applicants.

Many of the larger legal staffs are departmentalized. Therefore, don't just think of corporate law departments in the abstract — find out what they actually do. There are opportunities to do general corporate law, tax, labor relations, patent, trademark and copyrights, claims and litigation, anti-trust, contracts, real estate or international law. And since there will often be a senior attorney who heads a division that is concerned with a specific area, it helps to contact that person when your interests coincide with the work of her/his division.

Most corporate legal departments don't fill positions before there is an actual opening. Some insurance companies and banks recruit third-year students during the fall , and some corporations try to make early offers for patent attorney positions. But, by and large, corporations don't make prior commitments.

Therefore, don't panic if you can't find a corporate job by December of your third year of law school. In fact, you are probably better off spending the very early part of your third year researching the corporate job market — finding out which corporations have legal departments, which hire inexperienced lawyers, which make offers before graduation, and who is the best person in each law department for you to contact. Even those corporations that recruit in the fall at prestigious law schools will find themselves with positions to fill at the end of the school year and even after graduation. Job offers that they make are often simply not accepted. For example, about 50 corporations now interview at Harvard Law School each year, but only about 1 or 2% of each graduating class accepts positions with businesses. (Of about 500 graduates in the class of 1975 reporting, only about ten took jobs with corporations, and of about 420 graduates of the class of 1976 reporting, only three accepted positions with corporations.)

Finally, a word should be said about the efficacy of obtaining an M.B.A. for the purpose of making yourself more attractive to corporate hirers. If you seek the M.B.A. only as a credential to be considered for a legal position, save your time and money. If you are to be employed by the law department, your law background will be of primary interest. If, however, you have a real interest in business and hope to work in an other than strictly legal capacity — especially in a very small corporation where legal and business responsibilities are not so clearly delineated — then it would seem worthwhile to do graduate work in business administration. For an excellent overview of the structure and work of corporate legal departments, read *Law Practice in a Corporate Law Department*. This is a short pamphlet by the Committee on Corporate Law Departments of the ABA's Corporation, Banking and Business Law Section.

RESOURCES
Directories

The Corporate Council Roster. Although this directory was last published in 1972, and there are no plans for compiling a more recent edition, it can still be enormously helpful to you for identifying those corporations that have large law departments.

The directory contains an alphabetical listing of

corporations and includes the name of each attorney in the law department as well as some biographical information. Since much of the information is outdated, don't use the directory to find out the name of the general counsel of a corporation or any other official on the in-house counsel's staff. Instead, use *The Corporate Counsel Roster* to determine the relative size of a corporation's law department. Although most have grown in size since *The Roster* was published, most have grown proportionately, and therefore the size differential between the 50-attorney department and the ten-attorney one remains approximately the same.

In addition to discovering the size of the legal office, you will discover the organizational make-up, i.e. general law, patent, tax, international or labor relations. Or, you will learn that a particular corporation's legal office is not departmentalized at all. By looking at the titles of attorneys, or the sections of the ABA of which they are members, you get a very good sense of the scope of legal problems an in-house staff handles. Glancing through *The Roster* you repeatedly see the following areas mentioned: tax, claims, international, patent, trademark, copyright, labor relations, anti-trust, securities, title, unfair competition, product liability, contracts, real property and natural resources.

Finally, knowing *The Roster* was published in 1972, and then looking at the dates attorneys in different corporations were admitted to the bar, you can get a general sense of which corporate legal departments tend to hire recent graduates.

Martindale-Hubbell. Very few people ever think of using *Martindale* as a source for finding corporate law departments to contact. Although the information about corporations is not as easy to find as it is for private law firms, the front section of *Martindale* offers a wealth of leads to corporate counsels. Spend an hour going through the front section of attorneys in San Francisco, for instance.

By keeping a running tally of the number of times a corporation appears, it becomes clear that Pacific Gas & Electric Company has one of the largest — if not the largest — corporate law departments in San Francisco. It is apparent that other corporations with a substantial in-house legal staff include: Bank of America, Southern Pacific Transportation, Bechtel Corporation, Wells Fargo Bank, Standard Oil, Fireman's Fund Insurance, Pacific Telephone, Chevron, Crown Zellerbach and ITEL Corporation. A quick glance at the Patent Section reveals Chevron Research, Standard Oil of California and Crown Zellerbach as the companies listed most often.

Looking at the date of admission to the bar for each of the lawyers who work for the above-listed corporations, you see which ones hire recent graduates. Pacific Gas & Electric, for example, appears to hire a number of recent law graduates while Bechtel Corporation seems to have on-staff lawyers who have been out of law school and admitted to practice for a few years, at least.

Although they are not listed individually as often as any of the above companies, you see certain *kinds* of corporations that appear repeatedly. There are a number of leasing companies which are each listed three or four times. Perhaps this indicates something about the nature of the legal work of leasing companies, and that it's a good idea to contact other leasing companies to broach the possibility of your employment in the in-house legal department. In San Francisco, this same strategy is suggested for insurance companies, banks and trade associations by virtue of the number of them that employ at least some attorneys in-house.

Very often *Martindale* gives you the title of an attorney, and this will be helpful in determining the best person within a law department to contact. In addition to "general counsel," "general solicitor" or "counsel," *Martindale* delineates "vice-president and assistant general counsel," "assistant general counsel," "senior counsel" or, even, "senior tax counsel." Therefore, it is useful to use *Martindale* in conjunction with other resources that just indicate there is a law department but don't give any names, or give the name of the general counsel only. Or, as in the case of *The Corporate Counsel Roster*, where information about staff and titles might be out of date, *Martindale* can be used to corroborate information.

Industrial Directories. For the purpose of getting the names of some of the larger corporations, you can use the *Fortune Double 500 Directory* or the *College Placement Annual* (which also lists companies geographically and by occupation, e.g. law or banking and finance). However, none of these directories give information about the corporate legal department, and therefore must be used along with other resources.

Moody's Industrial Manual and Standard & Poor's Register of Corporations, Directors & Executives will usually give the name and title of at least the chief legal officer, e.g. "vice-president for legal affairs," "general counsel," "house counsel" or "counsel." Sometimes the person in charge of industrial relations, employee relations, labor relations, international operations or environmental affairs will also be indicated. Indexes for these directories are organized by industrial classification such as insurance, banks or title companies, and can easily be used to compile lists of places within particular industries.

Most state and regional trade associations publish their own industrial directories. Therefore, if your interests are within a specific geographic area, check directories for that location. The *Classified Directory of*

Wisconsin Manufacturers, the *Industrial Directory of Virginia*, the *Directory of New England Manufacturers*, the *Chicago, Cook County and Illinois Industrial Directory* or the *Southern California Business Directory and Buyers Guide* are examples of this kind of resource. They, like *Moody's* and *Standard & Poor's*, will often also give the name and title of the person responsible for legal matters.

Directories of Banks and Financial Institutions. There are several directories that list only banking, trust and other financial institutions. *Moody's Bank & Finance Manual* is one. Two excellent bank directories are the *Rand McNally International Bankers Directory* and *Polk's World Bank Directory.* Both usually give the name of the general counsel or head of the law department as well as the head of such departments as trusts or corporate finance — departments which are also likely to employ lawyers. You can then check *Martindale* to see if the heads of these departments are, in fact, lawyers themselves.

The *Directory of Trust Institutions*, published by *Trusts & Estates* magazine, lists bank trust departments and trust companies and gives the name of the trust officer or head of the trust department. Again, this name can be searched in *Martindale* to determine whether the person in charge of trust operations is an attorney.

Directories of Companies with Foreign Offices. Those who seek corporate legal department positions for the opportunity to practice international law or to work in another country will find two directories to be very helpful — the *Directory of American Firms Operating in Foreign Countries* and the *Directory of Foreign Firms Operating in the United States.* No information is given about the legal departments as such, but at least they provide names of firms that warrant being contacted for additional information about legal opportunities.

Other Sources

Continuing Legal Education Programs. Several of these programs run workshops dealing with issues related to corporate law, and the faculty who conduct these sessions often work on corporate in-house staffs. The brochures announcing these workshops list the participants and identify them with their corporate employer. Therefore, back and current issues of these brochures will provide you with leads to corporations and to lawyers within them. Good examples of the kind of sessions likely to give you such leads are the following, conducted in the past by the Practicing Law Institute: international banking, drug liability litigation, product liability litigation, employee benefits, trademark law, environmental regulation and litigation, anti-trust law, patent law, occupational safety and health, international taxation and securities litigation.

Professional Associations. The journals and directories of various professional associations of lawyers will give you clues to corporate employers. The American Bar Association Section on Corporation, Banking and Business Law puts out its own publication, *The Business Lawyer*. Each year the issue that follows the summer annual meeting of the A.B.A. includes a committee roster of the section. The name and address of each member of the section who serves on a committee is given. Although in most cases the actual name of the place where the member works is not given, it is given in enough cases to make this a valuable source for finding corporations that employ attorneys. And, in fact, for almost every member of the committees on Corporate Law Department Forums and Corporate Law Departments, the name of the firm where the member works is provided.

Go through either the *Encyclopedia of Associations* or *National Trade and Professional Associations of the U.S. & Canada*. Find those associations whose members include in-house lawyers, e.g. the Association of Life Insurance Counsel, the Association of Insurance Attorneys, American Patent Law Association or the Patent Office Society. Find out what publications are available and where and when conventions are held. The *Journal of the Patent Office Society*, for instance, not only includes articles by patent attorneys identified by where they work, but also lists job openings and those employment agencies that specialize in patent law placements. The National Association of College and University Attorneys (their work is really similar to the work of a corporate legal department) not only puts out the *College Law Digest* and the *Journal of College Law*, but it prepares a directory of its members as well.

Some associations might even operate placement services. The New York Patent Law Association tries to help graduates find patent positions, and has divided the responsibilities for placement between people in specific patent fields — chemical, mechanical and electrical.

The Wall Street Journal. Each Tuesday edition of *The Wall Street Journal* includes an extensive listing of job openings, many of which are legal positions. Most of the attorney positions require some years of experience, so the law student or very recent graduate should not look to the *Journal* for specific openings. Nevertheless, you can glean important information from it. You will discover those corporations that at least have some lawyers employed in-house, and even though a corporation is presently seeking an experienced attorney, this does not mean that they wouldn't also consider a recent graduate for another position at another time. You will also get a good sense as to the kind of work corporate attorneys do and the kinds of industries that repeatedly advertise for lawyers. You might not consider working for a trade association, for example, until you see the numbers that are looking to fill in-house attorney positions.

Private Employment Agencies. Since private agencies tend to be more active in recruiting for corporations than for law firms, it might be worthwhile to investigate this route. You still must contend with the "experienced only" restriction, however, as well as these agencies' Ivy League bias.

Since many corporations are under affirmative action pressures to hire women and members of minority groups, agencies might be particularly helpful to those who would be included under affirmative action programs. In fact, there are now a number of agencies that specialize in the placement of women in corporate positions, including law.

Judicial 9
Clerkships

"Selecting a law clerk is something like buying a car. I think these days very few people test drive a car for a week or so to determine all of its potentials or faults. Rather, they look at the upholstery, the color and the style, and seldom even bother to lift the hood. So it is with law clerks."

> A U.S. District Court judge
> commenting on the law clerk
> selection process

Law students tend to have a narrow view of the clerkship opportunities available to them. There are good federal judges outside of the Second, Ninth and District of Columbia Circuits! And there are good state court clerkships — even at the trial court level.

If, for example, you were to apply only to the U.S. Court of Appeals for the Second Circuit, you would be faced with the following situation. The 30 law clerks selected in 1976 represented only 12 schools (Harvard, Yale and Columbia accounting for 18 of the 30 clerkships). In 1975, only ten schools were represented by the 29 clerks selected (Harvard, Yale and Columbia accounting for 19 of the 29 clerkships).* Therefore, for those law students who don't have the luxury of top grades from the so-called top law schools, learning the full range of clerkship options becomes imperative.

Within the federal judiciary there are clerkship positions besides those with individual judges of the Courts of Appeals and District Courts. There are clerkships with the court, such as pro se clerk or motions clerk which can be as interesting as those with individual judges. Also, there are clerkships with the judges of the specialized courts like the U.S. Tax Court, U.S. Court of Claims or the U.S. Court of Customs and Patent Appeals. Outstanding performance in those areas related to the work of the special courts might be more important to these judges than simply your grades and school.

There are also a number of options within the state courts systems, on both the trial and appellate levels. In addition to offering clerkships with specific judges, many state courts have law departments which employ law graduates to serve as clerks for the entire court. Although you might be called a law assistant rather than a law clerk, and although you are serving all the judges rather than just one, the research and writing challenges and the total experience can be interesting and rewarding. Many state judges have their own law secretary, a more career oriented position than the typical one- or two-year clerkship. Though many of these law secretary positions are limited to admitted and experienced attorneys, there are exceptions. Therefore recent graduates should investigate these possibilities. And don't forget some of the specialized state courts — even juvenile courts in some jurisdictions offer opportunities for one- or two-year clerkships for graduates.

*This information was compiled by comparing articles printed in the *New York Law Journal* in 1975 and 1976 announcing the law clerks selected by federal judges in the Second Circuit.

Although there will be several exceptions, the following observations are generally true. Clerkships with courts in highly desirable geographic locations are more competitive; federal clerkships are harder to get than state court clerkships; appellate court clerkships are harder to get than ones with trial courts; and state courts tend to be more chauvinistic than federal courts in terms of choosing clerks who are from that state or who, at least, intend to practice there.

After you've determined the courts you are interested in, you then have to decide which judges on that court you want to apply to. Don't blindly apply to all judges. There are good and bad judges (including good judges who are bad to clerk for), and it's in your interest to make the effort to distinguish them. There is no one source you can look to, but the information is available. Most law school placement offices keep the comments and impressions of alumnae(i) who have clerked on file and accessible to students. Some of these reports are quite candid and thoughtful, and can be very helpful. Speak to former clerks and speak to faculty. Visit courthouses and speak to present clerks. Many are very approachable and can offer extraordinary insight into the clerking experience as well as give you information about specific judges. If you are interested in applying for a clerkship out-of-city or out-of-state, contact alumnae(i) or any other attorneys in that area and find out what they know about judges on the courts of that jurisdiction.

In addition, you should read the opinions of different judges and try to make your own assessment of the kinds of cases they handle (if some judge handles mostly anti-trust cases and that's your area of interest and experience, it would make sense to apply to her/him); their political leanings; and the level of craftsmanship. There is biographical information available about most judges (certainly federal judges), and if nothing else, it will help you find judges with whom you have some affinity (many judges hire clerks from the law schools where they have taught or studied).

In many places studies have been done that evaluate the performance of judges. *The Washingtonian* magazine, for instance, has published articles rating judges of the U.S. District Court for the District of Columbia, the District of Columbia Superior Court and the courts of the suburbs surrounding Washington. Jack Newfield's lists of "New York's Worst Judges" for the *New York Magazine* and *Village Voice* are well known.* Though the credibility of some of these surveys can be questioned, these ratings are perhaps most useful in identifying the most blatantly inferior judges. Whatever doubts these articles raise can be corroborated or dispelled by other sources, e.g. practicing attorneys. In the same way, some of the surveys rating judges conducted by bar association groups might be helpful to you. Several bar groups, including those in Connecticut, Washington state, Beverly Hills, Atlanta, Cleveland, San Francisco, Dallas and Chicago have rated judges. Not all of these surveys are available to the public, but some are. The results of the Connecticut survey were published in the newspaper. Inquire about the existence and availability of polls from the bar associations in those locales in which you are interested.

Since judicial clerkships are generally highly sought after (sometimes hundreds of applications will be received for one position), be realistic about your credentials. Aggravating the competitive situation even more is the fact that clerkship selections are still characterized by elitism and "established recruiting networks" (i.e. a judge, year after year, calling a former col-

*Harvey Katz, "Some Call it Justice," *The Washingtonian*, Sept. 1973; Jack Newfield, "The Ten Worst Judges in New York," *New York Magazine*, Oct. 16, 1972; and Newfield, "The Next 10 Worst Judges," *Village Voice*, Sept. 26, 1974.

league on a law school faculty and asking that person to recommend her/his best student). In 1976, 70% of the clerks judges selected came from the same school as the clerk who served in 1975! Regarding the Court of Appeals for the Second Circuit, in both 1975 and 1976 half the clerks selected came from the law school that was the alma mater of the judge for whom they were clerking. Although the findings for the judges on the U.S. District Court for the Southern and Eastern Districts of New York are not so dramatic, they still are suggestive. For both 1975 and 1976 almost one-third of the clerks chosen came from the same law school as the judge who selected her/him. And in 1976 about a third of the time a judge selected a clerk who graduated from the same school as the clerk being replaced.

Notwithstanding these hiring patterns — and they are being gradually knocked down — viable candidates for judicial clerkships should generally have excellent academic credentials (law review helps but it's certainly not imperative in every case). Also, since most clerkships are research and writing positions, applicants should demonstrate skill in these areas.

Therefore, applications to judges should indicate something about your academic standing and achievements and should include writing sample(s). Too many students think that only law review or other published articles constitute legitimate writing samples. This is not true. In fact, some judges discount articles that have been published in some periodical since they have usually been edited and re-edited a number of times. Also, since the problems that judges give clerks to research are real and pragmatic, many judges prefer to see writing about practical legal issues rather than something about abstract jurisprudential matters. Moot court briefs, papers for courses and memos for employers are often much better writing samples than published articles.

Recommendations, preferably from faculty, should

always follow your application. Most judges will insist upon getting some faculty input before selecting someone to be their clerk. Don't be gun-shy about asking faculty to recommend you. You don't have to be on a first name basis with a professor before you can ask for a recommendation. A few incisive comments in class during the course of a semester, an excellent paper or an A on an exam will often help a professor remember you.

There is usually no special application process involved in applying for clerkships. In most cases applications are sent directly to the judge you are interested in clerking for. In those cases where you are applying for a clerkship with the entire court, i.e. working as a law assistant in the court's law department, applications should be sent to the clerk of the court. Sometimes — usually at the state court level — an administrative office receives all resumes and then circulates them amongst the various judges who are seeking clerks and who have not themselves directly received applications. Some administrative offices collect applications and then arrange interviews for selected candidates before a panel of judges who will then pick their individual clerks from that pool.

Since most clerkships are for a definitive length of time — usually one or two years (two-year clerkships being much more common with federal judges) — openings can be anticipated and are usually filled months in advance of the time the clerkship will actually commence. Most federal clerkships are filled by the fall of each year for the following fall. That is, clerkships that commence in the fall of 1979, for example, would be filled by the fall of 1978. The American Association of Law Schools has attempted to get judges to delay receiving applications and interviewing until at least the beginning of the applicant's third year of law school. Despite these efforts, many federal judges still make their clerkship selections before the end of the summer and in some cases in the spring of the applicant's second year of law school . U.S. Court of Appeals judges seem to uniformly make early decisions.

To be safe, get your applications out by the end of your second year. Certainly apply by the end of the summer at the latest. If it turns out that you've applied too early, just remember to follow up on your application at the appropriate time.

At many schools there will be a clerkship committee that will coordinate the sending out of applications as will as recommendations. Often, clerkship committees screen applicants (often at the request of judges) and therefore only a limited number of students who wish to get the committee's endorsement actually do. If your school has a clerkship committee and you are able to get its support, use it for it will probably be helpful. However, don't let the committee do all the applying for you. Given the tremendous competition for clerkships, it is advisable to apply to a large number of judges, so make sure a clerkship committee doesn't leave you short. If your school has a clerkship committee but you don't get its backing despite your very good credentials, apply to judges on your own, regardless. There are countless examples of an applicant from a school who has applied to a judge directly and gotten a clerkship over the applicants recommended by the clerkship committee of the same school. In fact, there are many judges who prefer having applications sent directly from the applicant. These judges would simply prefer having an applicant, and not a committee, discover them.

If you have not secured a clerkship during the fall of your third year, all is not lost. There are still some judges who don't make selections until much later in the year, and some actually wait until the fall when the clerkship is to begin! Also, there are always new judges being appointed who then must find a clerk. Keep a lookout for new appointments. Read the papers that report legal news. Check the *U.S. Law Week,* which announces the retirement, death and appointment of federal judges. Sometimes even those judges who select early find themselves looking for a clerk late in the year because the person who originally accepted must give it up for some reason. So keep the word out that you are still interested in a clerkship and stay tuned to those sources that will lead you to late openings.

A final word about looking for a judicial clerkship should include some advice about interviews. Know why you are interested in clerking and why you are interested in a particular judge or court. Do some homework. Read the opinions of the judge with whom you have an interview scheduled. Talk to people about her/him. Presumably this was done when you were first deciding which judges to apply to, but in case it wasn't or in case your research was just perfunctory, certainly prepare again prior to your interview.

Resources

If you are seriously interested in finding out about the clerkship experience and the application process, read the series of articles in the *Vanderbilt Law Review,* Volume 26, November 1973. Almost the entire edition is devoted to "Judicial Clerkships: A Symposium on the Institution," which includes articles by federal and state judges as well as present and former clerks.

Listings of Judges

Federal. There are numerous sources that will give you the names of federal judges. None is particularly better than others, and the one(s) you use probably will depend upon their accessibility to you. The Administrative Office of the United States Courts has two directories which list all federal judges, including the Supreme Court, Courts of Appeals, District Courts and special courts like the Tax Court. They are the *United States*

Court Directory and the Register—Department of Justice and Courts of the United States. The United States Lawyers Reference Directory is an equally good source. If none of these directories are available, you can always get the names of federal judges from the front of a recent volume of the Federal Supplement or, for particular geographic locations, from a telephone directory under "United States Government—Courts."

Most of the above sources will give you a complete mailing address. If not, you can always rely on the following as being adequate: Honorable [Name], United States Court of Appeals for the [Circuit], United States Courthouse, [City, State, Zip]; or Honorable [Name], United States District Court for the [District], United States Courthouse, [City, State, Zip].

State. The National College of the State Judiciary publishes the Directory of State and Local Judges. This is a national listing which gives the name, address and phone number — state by state — of each judge on the state's court of last resort, intermediate appellate court, court of general jurisdiction and court of special/limited jurisdiction. The United States Lawyers Reference Directory, in addition to listing federal judges, lists the judges of each state's major courts.

Most states prepare their own publications giving information about that state's judiciary. Most state blue books, or their equivalent, will list state and local judges. The front of state reporters will also give the names of judges as will telephone directories.

It is important to know some biographical information about judges. It is helpful in deciding which judges to apply to and in preparing for interviews. In addition to newspaper articles (go, e.g., through the New York Times Index under the names of specific judges), there

Biographical Information About Judges

are a number of sources that will at least give you some rudimentary facts about a judge. The sources listed below typically will tell you when a judge was appointed and by whom (hint as to political affiliation); college and law school graduated from (from dates of graduation can determine approximate age); employment history prior to judgeship; and professional association memberships.

Federal. The *Biographical Dictionary of the Federal Judiciary* gives biographical information about all federal judges. If the *Dictionary* is not available to you, you can get the same information from *Who's Who in America* since it is from there that the information for the *Directory* is compiled.

There are usually books available that give you information about judges of a particular circuit. For instance, the *Second Circuit Redbook* provides biographical data for each judge on the Court of Appeals for the Second Circuit as well as each District Court judge for the Southern, Eastern, Western and Northern Districts of New York. The same information for federal judges in the District of Columbia Circuit can be found in the *Congressional Directory*. Also, *Who's Who in Government* includes all members of the federal judiciary.

State. In addition to federal judges, *Who's Who in Government* includes some state court judges. However, the books put out by each state about their judiciary are usually much more comprehensive. *California Courts and Judges* has biographical information for judges on California courts at all levels, from the California Supreme Court on down to the Municipal Courts. State blue books will at least list judges who are part of a state's judicial system, and in most cases will give some biographical information as well.

Graduate Law and Fellowship Programs

10

"Post-J.D. (or post-LL.B.) work is not useful for everyone. For example, students may well be disappointed if they come here with the notion that they can improve their academic credentials and thus obtain better jobs in large corporate law offices."

From a statement on the desirability of graduate law study prepared by the Committee on Graduate Studies of the Harvard Law School

Going to graduate school can fulfill many different needs. For some it's a chance to pursue areas of special interest developed during undergraduate law school. Or, it's an opportunity to study in a substantive field not included in an undergraduate law curriculum. Often, people do graduate work because it is a unique chance to do research under the supervision of a particular professor who is an expert in a field. For others, graduate school is a moratorium on making a job decision, or an interlude between jobs, or perhaps just a convenient way of getting situated in Berkeley, Cambridge, or New York.

There are presently about 40 law schools in the United States that give advanced degrees. The nature of these graduate law programs varies tremendously in size, quality and offerings. Some schools have very large programs. New York University, for instance, has more than 1,000 graduate students enrolled in its many programs. Other law schools with large graduate enrollments include Boston University, University of Florida, George Washington University, Harvard, Miami, Missouri at Kansas City, Southern Methodist University and Wayne State. Many law schools, however, have only a handful of graduate students enrolled. Chicago, Stanford, Texas or Cornell, for example, will usually have less than ten students at any one time working towards an advanced law degree. The bulk of the graduate law schools typically enroll between 20 and 40 students.

Some law schools allow graduate students great latitude in choosing their area of study. Schools such as Berkeley, Chicago, Columbia, Yale, Stanford, Michigan, Harvard or Virginia actually encourage applicants who have their own well-defined research interests. Other schools, however, might limit their graduate programs to very specific fields. Boston University and the University of Florida offer a LL.M. in Taxation only. Still other schools, although they don't limit their program to some one field of law, emphasize particular areas and attempt to attract students whose interests are in those fields. Examples of these graduate programs include Denver (Law and Society), Washington University (Taxation or Urban Studies), the University of Missouri (Urban Affairs) and Louisiana State (Marine Resources).

While most graduate programs offer only a LL.M., some offer both a LL.M. and a J.S.D. (this usually requires writing a dissertation). Some graduate programs are for full-time students only. Others accommodate large numbers of part-time graduate students, most of whom take courses during the evening. Although many graduate law schools are highly selective (especially the very small programs that seek people with definite research interests), some will admit most anyone who is a law school graduate, particularly if there is a part-time program. Each school, therefore, should be examined for its own requirements, offerings and resources. The sources listed at the end of the chapter will help you find this information.

Graduate study will probably be most satisfying to those who pursue it for more academic reasons than for the pragmatic purpose of simply obtaining a credential that will make you more saleable to employers. Generally, a LL.M. — and certainly a J.S.D. — is not looked at as a particularly useful credential in the minds of most employers. The exceptions are in the more specialized and technical areas of the law. A LL.M. in Taxation, for example, has come to be regarded as a positive credential by employers looking for tax attorneys. Perhaps if you wanted a fob related to environmental law issues involving the sea, a LL.M. in Ocean Law from the University of Miami might be helpful. However, it is doubtful that a LL.M. in Criminal Justice Studies will help you get a job with a public defender's office.

Even for those people contemplating a career in law school teaching, the utility of earning an advanced law degree as a credential is not clear. Most law professors at most law schools do not have graduate law degrees, and there does not seem to be any indication that advanced degrees will become any more important in the future hiring decisions of law schools. Law review membership at a top law school, followed by a federal clerkship and a few years' experience with a prestige firm is still the safest route.

Despite this general observation, there are still a

few graduate programs that probably will help someone who doesn't already have the "ideal credentials" to get a law teaching position. Harvard, Columbia and Yale claim to have been very successful in terms of their graduate students being able to get teaching jobs. For this reason, the graduate programs at these schools seem ideally suited for people with superior academic records from a less than absolute top-name school desiring to get jobs on law school faculties.

Generally, financial aid for graduate work is quite limited. A few schools give substantial amounts of financial aid to almost all of their graduate students. Most, however, give little or no financial assistance to students who wish to pursue graduate work, or they limit what little grant money they do give to foreign students. Financial aid for part-time graduate study is almost never granted by schools, although many employers will pay for graduate courses if they are related to the work of their office. Many law firms, for example, will pay for tax courses that associates take.

In addition to grants and loans, a few law schools have special fellowships for graduate study in a particular area which carry with them a sizeable stipend (often, tuition remission is given as well). New York University Law School provides a Food and Drug Law Institute Fellowship with a stipend of about $8,000 to do work for a LL.M. in Trade Regulation. NYU also has a Securities Institute Graduate Fellowship with a stipend of about $10,000 for graduate work leading to a LL.M. in Corporation Law. The Natural Resources Law Institute of Lewis and Clark Law School gives a $10,000 research/ teaching fellowship for graduate students to do specialized research in an area of Natural Resources Law. And the University of Pennsylvania School of Law gives fellowships in amounts up to about $12,500 for graduate students who work at its Center for the Study of Financial Institutions.

Teaching Fellowships, Instructorships or Assistantships. Several law schools provide opportunities for recent law graduates to teach first-year legal research and writing (often including appellate advocacy) or to supervise students in the school's clinical law program. In some instances this teaching fellowship is in addition to doing graduate work. At other schools the graduate study is optional, and at some law schools there is no opportunity at all for teaching fellows or assistants to do graduate work. Certain teaching fellowships try to attract graduates who are interested in a teaching career. Most simply attempt to find law graduates with good academic records, excellent research and writing skills, and a wish to spend a year or two developing materials and teaching legal research.

Some Specific Graduate Opportunities

The following are examples of schools that provide graduate law study opportunities to teaching fellows: George Washington (Teaching Fellowship Program); Temple (Law and Humanities Fellowship Program); Harvard (Law Teaching Fellowship Program); NYU (Instructorships in Law); Columbia (Associates-in-Law Program); Stanford (Legal Research and Writing Instructorships); and Illinois (Law Teaching Fellowship Program). Many of these programs publicize themselves as being for graduates who wish to ultimately find regular teaching positions. The University of Wisconsin Law School, in fact, offers Minority Group Law Graduate Fellowships (entails counseling students rather than teaching research and writing) specifically to black, Chicano, Puerto Rican or native American law graduates who contemplate a teaching career.

Many other schools offer teaching assistantships although there is no opportunity to do graduate work as well. Examples are: Arkansas, Boston College, Suffolk, Delaware, Cincinnati, Toledo, Catholic University, and the University of Puget Sound.

Instead of offering fellowships to teach legal research and writing, the following law schools offer the chance to teach in the school's clinical program: Temple (Clinical Teaching Fellowship); Georgetown (Institute for Public Interest Representation); Denver (Clinical Education Fellowships); Loyola of Los Angeles (Graduate Teaching Fellowship); Antioch (Graduate Teaching Fellowship Program); Pennsylvania (Criminal Law and Litigation Program).

Typically, these research and writing or clinical fellowships carry stipends ranging between about $9,000 and $13,000. Considering that this is usually for a nine-month academic year, and often some part is characterized as a research stipend and is tax exempt, these fellowships pay very well. Also, where graduate work is pursued in addition to teaching, tuition remission is usually provided.

*Graduate Study in Foreign Countries.*There are a few American law schools that give a LL.M. for work that partially entails study at a foreign university. The Jervey Fellowship Program in Foreign Law at Columbia Law School is approximately a two-year program, the first of which is spent at Columbia and the second at a European university of the fellowship holder's choice. The Georgetown Institute for International and Foreign Trade Law offers a two-year fellowship to study legal aspects of international trade, investment, development and multinational corporations. One year is spent studying at Georgetown and the other in Germany.

In addition, there are literally scores of foreign law schools that have graduate programs that are open to American law school graduates. Aside from the obvious opportunities to study international and comparative law, there are course offerings in most substantive areas of the law, including a number of programs in criminology. Many of the foreign law schools are in English-speaking countries, so language requirements should not be a barrier. Australia, Canada, Ireland, India, New Zealand, South Africa, England and Scotland all have law schools with substantial graduate programs.

Although financial assistance from a foreign law school is usually hard to come by, tuition at many foreign schools is minimal — certainly when compared to tuition at American law schools. A year's tuition at a British law school would amount to less than $1,000.

Fellowships in Settings Other Than Law Schools. Some universities (other than in their law schools) have graduate programs that would be of interest to law school graduates. At the University of Massachusetts, for example, the Labor Relations and Research Center offers a Master of Science degree in Labor Studies. Cornell has post-doctoral associateships to study the relationship between the humanities, science and technology. This program attempts to attract people with a specific interest in researching problems concerned with environmental law and ethics, and it considers law school graduates. The University of Pittsburgh has a graduate program in Health Law offered jointly by the School of Public Health and the School of Law.

Institutions other than schools sometimes give fellowships for special kinds of research or work. The Russell Sage Foundation has a Law and Social Science Residency Program which grants stipends for a year or two for people to do research involving the application of the social sciences to some field of law. The American Civil Liberties Union Foundation has a Marvin Karpatkin Fellowship to enable a recent law graduate to work in its national office in New York City for a year. The Center for Law in the Public Interest in Santa Monica, California also gives a fellowship to allow someone to work in this non-profit public interest law firm. The Earl Warren Legal Training Program gives fellowships to a small number of recent black law graduates to spend a year as an intern doing Civil Rights Law. Following this one-year internship, Fellows receive retainers for three years — on a diminishing basis — to help them set up a private practice "where there is either no friendly lawyer or where severe shortage exists in relation to the needs of the local black population."

There are even some fellowship opportunities to work in other countries. The International Bureau of Fiscal Documentation in Amsterdam offers a few one-year fellowships (which can be renewed for a second year) to recent law graduates to work on its journals concerning issues of comparative taxation. The International Council of Environmental Law in Bonn, Germany, also has a research fellowship which, among other responsibilities, includes working on its publication, *Environmental Policy and Law*. Although there is no single place you can look which will publicize these or other programs, most will send literature to law school placement offices. Also, if you discover one program, someone connected with it will probably be aware of similar programs in other places.

RESOURCES   Most graduate and fellowship programs send literature, or at least announcements, to law school placement offices. Many law schools that have graduate programs prepare catalogs and brochures describing them, and you should write directly to schools to get a copy. Usually there will be someone on a law school faculty or a member of the administration who is knowledgeable about graduate study, and you should seek such persons out. In addition, the directories listed below should give you leads to where to write to get information.

Graduate Law Study: Directory of Graduate Law Programs Offered Throughout the World. This directory summarizes the major features of law graduate programs at law schools in the United States as well as in other countries. For each school it lists the degrees offered, admission requirements, application deadline, curriculum, special areas of study, fellowships, tuition, number of graduate students currently enrolled, the number of credits that can be taken in graduate courses outside the law school, and whether or not there is an evening program.

Although the *Directory* is very comprehensive, the information — especially for the curriculum — is only a summary, and therefore you should always write directly to a school for fuller descriptions. Nevertheless, this book gives an excellent overview of what is available, and where, and is a very good initial source to consult.

Survey and Directory of Clinical Legal Education 1975-1976. This *Directory*, prepared by the Council on Legal Education for Professional Responsibility, summarizes various aspects of clinical legal education programs at American law schools. Although most of the information will not be of direct interest to people investigating graduate law opportunities, there is a section that will give you leads to those law schools that use graduate students to help supervise their clinical program.

"Table 6: Clinical Supervision By Law School Staff or Faculty" gives the title of supervising attorneys. Where "lecturer," "instructor," "clinical fellow," "graduate fellow," "intern," "graduate intern," or "teaching fellow" is listed, the school probably uses recent law school graduates to help supervise second- or third-year students enrolled in their clinical programs. In many instances, graduates hired to work in a school's clinical program are also given the opportunity to pursue their own graduate study at the same time.

Alternative **11** Careers

Throughout history lawyers, from Cicero to Geraldo Rivera, have won recognition for their non-legal endeavors. Lawyers who are known for their achievements in "alternative careers" include Sir Thomas More, Copernicus, Descartes, Tchaikovsky, Lenin, Ghandi, Castro, Jules Verne, Paul Robeson, Francis Scott Key and Howard Cosell!

Although law graduates have often gone into professions totally unrelated to the law, this chapter discusses alternative careers that follow somewhat logically from a law school education. They are endeavors that are alternative to the practice of law per se, but they are professions for which a legal education is useful and law graduates particularly well qualified. In fact, for some of the positions a law degree might even be required.

Law students tend to be much more open-minded about what they might do with their law degree at the time they enter law school than by the time they graduate. Somehow the law school experience induces people to become litigators. However, it's important to realize that a law degree is not wasted just because you don't use it in a traditional way. There are many non-law jobs in which your legal skills will be of tremendous benefit, and these jobs can be as interesting and challenging as the practice of law itself. Some years ago, Brandeis University actually contemplated starting a law school for people who would not practice law. It was to be a school for social scientists, administrators and other policy-makers who could better perform their work by learning some law and obtaining the analytical and problem-solving skills of lawyers.

In the context of a tight job market, it becomes even more important for law students to remain open to the alternative ways of using their degree. And it is the responsibility of law schools to actively recruit students whose plans are other than to become practicing attorneys.

SUPERVISORY POSITIONS	A legal education is a good background for various kinds of administrative positions with businesses, universities, foundations, unions, social service organizations and community groups. Many administrators now working in these settings are law graduates themselves.

There have always been a large number of law graduates who have found their way into management or supervisory positions in companies. Usually these are people whose interests are in the day-to-day operation of a business as opposed to a more limited interest in its legal affairs only. Often, these law graduates have had a business training prior to law school. Many have already obtained a Masters in Business Administration, while others get the M.B.A. after law school. There are even a number of law schools now that have combined J.D.-M.B.A. programs in which one is able to earn both these degrees during a four-year period.

Sometimes the product a company manufactures or sells, as well as the potential clients who create a market for a product, makes it essential that its management personnel, including salespeople, have a legal education. For example, there are companies that sell computerized legal research equipment that seek law graduates for their executive, sales and training positions. Legal publishing companies also would be interested in executives with legal training, since lawyers and law firms comprise the major buyers for their products and services.

Lawyers, in great numbers, have come to assume various administrative posts within universities. There is an inordinately large number of law graduates who are presidents of colleges and universities! Lawyers are found at all levels of university administration — as deans, assistant deans and special assistants — with responsibility over all phases of running a school (though usually confined to non-academic matters). A law background seems particularly attractive in areas related to affirmative action programs, employee relations and development or fund raising. Many law school administrators responsible for admissions, alumnae(i) affairs and placement are themselves law graduates.

In the past several years a great many colleges and universities have created the position of ombudsman. Since this position requires setting up procedures for the receipt and resolution (including negotiation and arbitration) of student, faculty and staff complaints and grievances, a law background would be ideal.

Foundations employ people with law degrees. Several law graduates are executive directors of foundations, expecially the smaller ones. Many of the large foundations (i.e. Ford, Rockefeller, or Carnegie) employ law graduates in different capacities, including program officials who review, develop and help implement projects funded by these foundations.

Unions also hire lawyers for positions other than in their legal departments. Many officers of unions are lawyers. Law graduates work as organizers for unions, head pension funds, administer health benefit programs and handle governmental relations.

International, national and regional social service organizations hire law graduates for administrative positions. Those organizations whose programs are sensitive to federal and state legislation would probably be the most interested in finding law graduates. Examples of such organizations include those dealing with the problems of health care, alcoholism, cruelty to children, population control, consumerism and adoption.

Community groups also provide many opportunities for people to use their law school skills — especially those whose activities involve dealing with legislatures, the police and the courts. Lawyers are well prepared to assume the administrative, organizing and fund-raising responsibilities of the following types of community organizations: tenant groups, health programs (e.g. Health Policy Advisory Committees), citizen action groups (e.g. the Nader-affiliated Public Interest Research Groups, or PIRGs as they are more commonly known), consumer groups, drug abuse programs, community arbitration and mediation centers (which settle complaints as an alternative to a court action), as well as other court and jail diversion programs.

TEACHING   Law graduates teach law and law-related courses on both a full-time and part-time basis in schools at all levels. Colleges and universities have lawyers on their political science and business school faculties. They typically teach courses in law and society, the legal system, constitutional law, business law, tax accounting and corporate taxation. There are now literally hundreds of schools (especially community or junior colleges) that have criminal justice or law enforcement departments. These programs are for students who are presently, or plan to become, police or other law enforcement officers — people who will work for police, probation and parole departments. These programs seem to be very receptive to hiring law graduates to teach courses relating to the criminal justice system, including courses in constitutional law, criminal law and criminal procedure.

Many high schools, junior high schools and even elementary schools now have special programs in legal education as part of their curriculum. Aside from teaching these courses to students, there are opportunities for lawyers to develop the substantive content of them, set them up and train other teachers.

Other teaching opportunities for law graduates include the many paralegal or legal assistants' programs that have been started in recent years. The curriculum for these programs includes many of the same substantive law courses taught in the first two years of law school. Even schools for court reporting seek law graduates to teach certain parts of their curriculum.

RESEARCH

There are scores of programs, usually foundation or government funded, that conduct studies, publish reports, and develop and implement projects in legal and related areas. Their staffs often include lawyers. For instance, there are research centers all over the country that do studies relating to the criminal justice system, with particular emphasis on court reform. The Vera Institute of Justice (New York City), the Institute of Judicial Administration (at NYU Law School), Fund for Modern Courts (New York City), and the American Judicature Society (Chicago) are examples of these programs. Also, every state and most large localities have criminal justice coordinating councils or crime control planning boards. Although their names vary, they all serve the same purpose of distributing federal Law Enforcement Assistance Administration (LEAA) funds for various criminal justice related projects. Often, lawyers are employed by these agencies as researchers, analysts and planners who review, develop, implement and evaluate projects. Many of the court-monitoring projects that have been conducted were funded by these agencies, and staff people with law degrees have often overseen them.

Other research centers have much more generalized interests, but still hire law graduates for their projects involving legal policy studies. "Think tanks" such as the Hudson Institute (New York), Urban Institute (Washington, D.C.), the Center for Women Policy Studies (Washington, D.C.) and the Rand Institute (California) are places that do studies for which a knowledge of the law is helpful.

Nader-affiliated programs have employed countless numbers of law graduates over the years to conduct their studies and write their reports. The Corporate Accountability Research Group, Health Research Group and Tax Reform Research Group are some obvious examples.

CONSULTING   Many private consulting firms hire people with law degrees. Firms that consult corporate management might want someone with legal training. This would be more likely if the specific subject of consulting involved such matters as estate planning, pension and other employee benefit plans, taxes or governmental relations.

LOBBYING   Because of their knowledge of laws, legislation and the legislative process, it would be natural that lawyers be employed as lobbyists. Aside from representing broad-based citizen groups such as Common Cause or the Nader-affiliated Congress Watch, lobbyists are employed by political organizations, trade associations for various industries or groups of manufacturers, corporations (especially large companies that have huge federal contracts), state and local governments, unions and an infinite range of other interest groups whose activities and concerns are affected by legislation.

ACCOUNTING

The tax departments of the large public accounting firms usually employ several law school graduates. In fact, many of the "Big Eight" accounting firms engage in very active on-campus recruiting at law schools. (The "Big Eight" include Peat, Marwick, Mitchell & Co.; Arthur Andersen; Ernst & Ernst; Haskins & Sells; Price Waterhouse; Coopers & Lybrand; Touche, Ross & Co.; and Arthur Young.)

Those accounting firms that hire lawyers, for the most part, look for people with accounting backgrounds (preferably an undergraduate degree in accounting) to work as tax accountants in their tax departments or sometimes as management consultants. The starting salaries and partnership opportunities in the large accounting firms compare very favorably with those in law firms, including many of the large, prestigious corporate law firms.

LAW PUBLISHING

Publishers of law books and the many legal reporting services hire lawyers for their editorial staffs. In some companies almost the entire editorial staff of researchers and writers will be law graduates. Among the largest of the law publishing companies are the following: West

Publishing (Minneapolis and Long Island), Commerce Clearing House (Chicago), the Bureau of National Affairs (Washington, D.C.), Prentice-Hall (New Jersey), Matthew Bender (New York City and San Francisco), Callaghan & Co. (Chicago) and The Lawyers Cooperative Publishing Co. (Rochester) which includes their subsidiaries, Bancroft-Whitney (San Francisco) and the Research Institute of America (New York City).

In addition there are various legal periodicals that might be interested in hiring law graduates, although their staffs are usually quite small. *Trusts & Estates* or *Tax Journal* are examples of the kind of magazine that potentially would want to hire lawyers.

LAW LIBRARIES

Law schools, courts, bar associations, government agencies and large private law firms all have libraries that require full-time personnel. The head law librarian is very often (and at law school libraries almost always) a law graduate. Many law librarians, in addition, have a Masters of Library Science degree (M.L.S.).

The duties of law librarians are often combined with other responsibilities. Law librarians at law schools usually teach courses in legal research and writing. Bar association librarians might have responsibility for planning legal education programs or for writing newsletters and other association publications.

RESOURCES

Since the alternatives to practicing law are limitless, the possible resources available for ideas and information are limitless as well. The most important thing is to be open to the possibility of using your legal education in a way other than as a practitioner.

Browse through journals, magazines, newsletters

and newspapers. Go through law school alumnae(i) directories and then contact those graduates who have opted for some profession besides the practice of law, but who have, nevertheless, utilized their legal training. They are likely to have some good ideas and to know other law graduates who similarly have opted for an alternative to the practice of law.

Some of the more obvious resources related to the kinds of alternative careers mentioned in this chapter are listed below.

BUSINESSES

Many of the same resources listed in the chapter on Corporations will be useful for finding places to contact concerning administrative or non-legal executive positions. Among the sources listed for that chapter, *Martindale-Hubbell*, *The Wall Street Journal* and the various industrial directories (i.e. *Moody's* or *Standard & Poors*) should prove to be particularly useful.

UNIVERSITIES

The New York Times. Section 4 of the Sunday *Times* includes an extensive list of university administrative positions (including law school positions) under "Careers in Education."

The Chronicle of Higher Education. This is a weekly publication which lists teaching and administrative positions available in colleges and universities throughout the country, and even some listings for positions abroad. This is perhaps the single most comprehensive source for university administration openings.

The Spokeswoman. This publication of women-related activities includes a classified ad section in which there is usually a number of listings for administrative positions. Universities are attempting to affirmatively hire women.

FOUNDATIONS

The Foundation Directory. This directory lists and describes the major foundations in the United States (in terms of their endowment). The name of the executive director, secretary or other appropriate contact person is also listed. It lists the purpose and activities of each foundation. Therefore, to find foundations that might be interested in someone with a law degree, look for those that fund law-related social action programs. The description of the Ford Foundation, for example, includes the following programs: civil rights and civil liberties; social, political and economic equality; legal education reform; research, training and experiments in legal services for the poor, corrections and criminal law; judicial administration and public interest law.

Foundation Grants Index. To find those foundations that fund law-related projects, go through the *Index* under such headings as "Criminal Justice," "Corrections," "Courts," "Crime," and "Law Enforcement."

UNIONS

Directory of National Unions and Employee Associations. This lists national unions and gives the names of officials and heads of various departments (e.g. Government Relations).

Also, refer to those additional resources discussed under unions in Chapter 7, Public Interest.

SOCIAL SERVICE ORGANIZATIONS AND COMMUNITY GROUPS

Encyclopedia of Associations and *Information Resources for Public Interest*. These are both excellent sources for finding organizations and groups all over the country. Although *Information Resources* has a much broader scope and includes many more kinds of institutions, it gives much less information about each entry than the *Encyclopedia*.

Teaching

Those sources listed above under University Administration also have teaching openings. These sources are the Sunday *New York Times, The Chronicle of Higher Education* and *The Spokeswoman*. In addition, the following sources should be consulted.

Placement Bulletin, Association of American Law Schools. This newsletter, published six times an academic year, lists faculty openings at both ABA approved and unapproved law schools. There are also a few college and university law-related positions announced in each issue.

The AALS also maintains a directory of people looking for law teaching jobs, and for a fee you can have your resume included in this directory which is circulated among law schools looking to fill faculty vacancies. In addition, the AALS holds two conventions each year, one of which is solely for the purpose of faculty recruiting.

Survey and Directory of Clinical Legal Education 1975-1976. For those looking for teaching positions in law school clinical programs, this is an excellent resource. It lists all law schools that have clinical programs and gives information about each one, including its staff size, student enrollment and the areas of the law it involves.

Law Enforcement and Criminal Justice Education—Directory. This book lists all colleges and universities (including two-year and four-year schools and under-graduate programs) that offer courses in criminal justice studies. The size of the program, in terms of both student enrollment and staff size, and the courses offered are detailed for each school. This is an invaluable source for anyone with the specific interest of teaching in this kind of program.

Research   *Research Centers Directory.* This includes research centers throughout the country. However, its emphasis seems to be on those research programs that are affiliated with universities.

Foundation Grants Index. Since most research projects are foundation funded, going through back issues of the *Index* will uncover most of the major programs. Look in the index under "Corrections," "Criminal Justice" or "Court Reform," for example.

National Center for State Courts Annual Report. Since many law-related research projects entail studying various aspects of court reform, this annual report should be quite helpful. It summarizes those court-related studies that are funded by the Center as well as by other sources.

Various Reports of Criminal Justice or Crime Control Planning Boards. These are the agencies through which flow federal funds for criminal justice projects. Therefore, their reports will list and describe the projects they fund, many of which will include court, juvenile justice and adult criminal justice research studies.

Consulting   *Consultants and Consulting Organizations Directory.* By looking in the subject index under "estate planning," "pension planning," "tax," "government relations" and other law-related headings, it is easy to compile a list of those consulting companies that are likely to be interested in someone with a law background.

Directory of Registered Federal and State Lobbyists. **Lobbying**
This lists lobbyists and the organization or company they represent. In addition to an alphabetical listing, there is a listing state by state. It is easy to tell at a glance which groups or companies are represented by the largest number of lobbyists.

Compiling a list of accounting firms, especially the **Accounting** largest ones, should be quite simple. Most anyone familiar with accounting firms will know the "Big Eight." The *College Placement Annual* lists most of the major accounting firms. Talk to someone who teaches in a business school or contact someone in a university placement office who has responsibility for business placements. Any of these people will probably have access to a list of accounting firms.

Browsing through any law library will quickly reveal **Law** the major publishers of law books and reporting ser- **Publishing** vices. Also, an article in the February, 1974 issue of *Juris Doctor*, entitled "Lawbook Publishing: A $145 Million-a-Year Business," lists and describes the major law publishing companies.

The New York Times. The Sunday *Times* has a separate **Law** "Librarian Openings" section under "Careers in Educa- **Librarianship** tion." Many of the positions that are available are in law libraries.

Directory of Law Libraries. This is a comprehensive listing of most every law library in the United States.

Directory of Special Libraries and Information Centers. Although this directory is not limited to law libraries, it is quite easy to pick them out. The index gives a state by state listing under the subject heading "law libraries."

American Association of Law Libraries. Among its other activities, this professional association has recently created a Placement Committee which attempts to match law library openings with qualified people looking for such positions.

Summer and Part-time Jobs

12

"We're looking for smart people. We couldn't care less whether someone is a first or second year student."

An administrator of a summer program for a U.S. Attorney's Office

"First-year students should not call on the law firms concerning summer employment without first consulting the Placement Office, since most large and medium sized law firms do not offer summer clerkships to first year students.

From "Interviewing Procedures For Law Students and Prospective Employers," a statement of principles agreed to by law schools and New York City large and medium firms

Most everything that has been discussed in this book in terms of opportunities available, approaches to job markets, and resource materials, applies to summer and part-time jobs. This chapter, however, will talk about such jobs as strategies in themselves for getting full-time positions upon graduating from law school.

Probably the most common question asked of placement offices by law students is, "What should you do about getting a job if you're not in the top of your class or on law review?" The answer is simple. Plan to work for a place throughout law school which will offer you a job after graduation, based on your work performance rather than your resume. Plan to have your full-time offer evolve from an on-going work relationship. Initially, get your foot in the door any way you can. Volunteering during your second year of law school can lead to a paying job that summer, which can lead to a full-time job offer when you graduate.

The importance of part-time and summer positions in the evolution of a full-time job cannot be over-stressed. The Placement Office at Northeastern University School of Law in Boston (whose cooperative program requires that law students alternate semesters of coursework with those of legal employment) estimates that about 40% of the full-time job offers made to its graduates each year grow out of the co-op placements.

It is well known that the large corporate firms run summer programs as an integral part of their full-time recruiting efforts, each year making the major portion of their full-time offers to the summer associates of the past summer. If a small firm has had a law student working for them as a clerk, in most cases any full-time offer that is made goes to that person. Many government agencies recruit from their summer programs as well. One federal agency, which consistently hires nine or ten graduates a year, gets these new lawyers from the pool of 15 or 16 students who worked for the agency during the summer. In effect, the summer program has totally eliminated the need for this agency to recruit third-year students for permanent positions.

For a recent graduate to get a job with certain public interest law employers, a prior, on-going work experience there is sometimes the only way. Chapter 7 on Public Interest emphasized this fact. This is especially true of the small, highly sought-after public interest law firms. And although it might not be so critical in regards to larger and less selective public interest employers, working during law school makes things a lot easier. For example, a criminal defenders program which hires about 30 recent graduates a year estimates that about a third of the offers go to people who have worked for them as interns during law school. Even in obtaining a judicial clerkship, working for that judge during law school can be determinative. There are a number of law schools which now have judicial clinical programs which allow their students to clerk for federal judges and receive law school clinical credit. These schools have reported a substantial correlation between participating in this clinical experience with a particular judge and getting a full-time judicial clerkship with that judge after graduation.

Despite the commonly accepted pessimism amongst law students regarding the availability of summer jobs, there happen to be a great many opportunities. They just don't all pay $450 a week! Large- and medium-sized firms have summer associates programs which can number from five to 20 or more law students. Although small firms don't necessarily hire law students in predictable numbers every summer, many small firms, including one- and two-attorney offices, take on summer help. In fact, in certain respects small firms rely upon summer and part-time hiring more than larger firms. A large firm will have a number of associates (or the ability to hire more) that can handle increases in workload due to new cases or people going on vacation. A small firm doesn't have that ability, and therefore depends a lot more on law student assistance to cope with increased workloads.

The summer programs of many publicly funded employers have suffered in recent years due to government fiscal crises and budget cutbacks. The federal agencies have probably been the least affected, compared to state and local legal staffs. Almost every federal agency hires some law students for the summer. A few agencies hire large numbers of students for their very extensive summer internship programs. The Justice Department and the Chief Counsel's Office of the Internal Revenue Service, for instance, both hire about 100 law students each summer. There are several agencies that hire between ten and 20 law students each summer to work in Washington, D.C. (regional offices often hire some students as well, but usually hire autonomously from Washington). Among those agencies with medium-sized programs are: Customs (Office of Regulations and Rulings); Federal Trade Commission; Federal Communications Commission; Health, Education and Welfare; Securities and Exchange Commission; Housing and Urban Development Administration; General Accounting Office; and the General Services Administration. All other federal agencies with legal staffs will hire at least one, two or three students, although they will not be hired as part of a structured summer program as such.

Many state and local agencies have kept their summer law programs despite economic difficulties, but have often resorted to paying small stipends or hiring volunteers only. The worth of these opportunities remains even though they pay little or no salary, and if it is financially possible for you to work under those circumstances, you should. A better-paying summer job might not be nearly as worthwhile in terms of experience or as an entree to a full-time job. Attorneys general's offices and district attorneys' offices are two good examples of places that frequently pay a small stipend only, but remain as excellent summer opportunities.

Financial difficulties have affected the summer programs of many foundation-supported projects as well. Those that have continued are often unique summer employment opportunities that should be pursued despite relatively small amounts of compensation. The Law Students Civil Rights Research Council (LSCRRC) has for a number of years provided summer jobs in civil rights offices all over the country. Now the LSCRRC internships are primarily for black law students in the South to work in civil rights offices and programs in that part of the country. The National Lawyers Guild also runs a summer program. In recent summers the Guild has hired law students to work for projects all over the country involving such issues as the following: housing, police brutality, immigration, and the rights of farmworkers, Indians, blacks, women, coal miners and prisoners.

Regarding both publicly funded and foundation-funded programs, law students should investigate the possibility of qualifying for the federal work-study program. Under this program the federal government provides funds to colleges and universities to pay the major portion of the salaries of those students who qualify and who work either for government agencies or non-governmental, non-profit organizations. Typically, work-study funds will cover 80% of a student's salary, the remaining 20% is paid by the employer. If the salary is between $3 and $4 an hour, an employer gets the services of a law student for between 60 cents and 80 cents an hour! The attractiveness of this arrangement often persuades an organization to take on a law student for the summer, or during the school year, when otherwise it could never be considered. The Urban Corps programs in New York City, Washington, D.C. and Atlanta, for example, place large numbers of law students who are on work-study in city agencies which otherwise would have had no ability to hire law students. Many legal services programs, criminal defenders offices and prosecutors' offices hire almost exclusively work-study students.

Check to see if your school has a work-study program and one that is open to law students. Since qualifying for the program is based solely on financial need, many law students who are financially independent of their parents easily qualify with a very high economic need priority.

A law school's externship program is another vehicle that is often used by law students as a means to work in a particular place. Under these programs a student works outside the law school but receives law school credit for that work. Sometimes it will entail working a few hours a week for a couple of credits. In other situations it might entail working full-time for an entire semester in another part of the country and receiving a full semester's worth of law school credit. Or, as is the case with Northeastern's Co-op Program, students can receive both credit and a salary.

There are certain employers that actually give preference to summer job applicants who can stay on after the summer. Therefore, externship programs can be used as leverage for getting a summer position. If the possibility of an externship is not available to you, try to extend good summer jobs into the school year on some other basis, whether it be part-time for pay, independent study or volunteering. Although it might be more convenient to work during the school year in your law school's library, in terms of getting a job when you graduate, it's worth the effort to extend summer jobs into the school year to make them on-going. This should certainly be done for those summer jobs you enjoyed, at places where you would like to work when you graduate. Similarly, good part-time jobs should be made on-going into the following summer.

Summer jobs in law settings are available to people after their first year of law school. First-year students are too ready to accept the myth that it's next to impossible to get a law job after your first year, so don't even try. Nonsense! A large percentage of any first-year class can, and does, find legal work during the summer. This is certainly the case at those schools where there is an extensive work-study program.

Many employers don't draw any distinction between first- and second-year students. Summer jobs require a lot of legal research and writing and a lot of legwork. Second-year students are not that much more prepared to do this. Since many students do no legal research and writing during their second year, their experience is limited to their first-year writing assignments anyway. Employers that limit their summer hiring to second-year students often do so because their summer program is used to recruit students for full-time jobs for the following year, and not because only second-year students have the ability to perform the tasks of a summer associate.

Small firms are the most likely source of summer jobs for first-year students. But even the large corporate firms that presumabley hire only second-year students for the summer do, from time to time, hire first-year students. Often, they will hire a first-year student but not necessarily as part of their regular summer associates program. A firm might have a special project for which they would hire first-year students — perhaps a large antitrust case or a corporate stock offering, both of which require hours of paper gathering. If you are especially interested in a job as a first-year student, apply and don't be put off from the start by the "second-year only" or "second-year preferred" caveats.

Finally, don't forsake the summer job quest simply because you have not found something towards the end of the school year. With the exception of those firms that recruit during the fall, most firms don't decide to hire students for the summer much in advance of the time school ends. Many, in fact, hire after the summer break has already begun.

Even the government agencies that hire law students each summer often don't decide until May or June how many positions they will fill. Many agencies wait until this time, which is close to the end of their fiscal year, to determine how extensive a summer program their budget will allow. Once the decision to hire is made, an agency must fill positions in a hurry. Since there is usually a backlog of applications and no ability to quickly determine who is still available and interested, offers are often made to those who just happen to apply or reapply around that time. Many Washington, D.C. area law students have gotten jobs with agencies simply because they were there. Therefore, if you've applied to a government agency in the early part of the school year and have not heard from them, contact them again to register your continued interest. Certainly, you should make overtures in May or even June after school finishes — ideally by going to Washington.

This same strategy is valid regarding private firms, public interest employers and any other place to which you have applied but have not heard from. At most law schools, probably a third to a half of the summer jobs secured are found in May and June. That is not to say you should wait until then to start looking for summer work. It is only to say that despite your efforts throughout the school year, if you are still looking at the beginning of the summer, you should know that many summer jobs are still available in law settings at that time. You don't have to accept a camp counselor's position in May out of desperation.

RESOURCES   All of the resources mentioned in prevous chapters are as relevant to finding a summer job or part-time position as they are to securing a full-time job. You should certainly read each chapter about those work settings that are of interest to you.

In addition, the resources listed below should be

especially useful in looking for summer or part-time jobs.

Harvard Law School Public Interest Questionnaire. This resource was discussed in the Public Interest chapter. It is listed again now, because it is particularly useful for finding summer jobs. The questionnaire specifically asks if a place hires for the summer, how many openings are anticipated, the pay, if any, and whether they consider first-year students.

The *Questionnaire* does an excellent job of delineating those places that take on work-study students, either as a preference or exclusively.

Summer Jobs — Opportunities in the Federal Government. Since most placement offices have this book, put out by the U.S. Civil Service Commission, a word should be said about it. That word is "caution." The information in this book is too general to be of much help. Use it as a starting point, at most. Many more agencies than it lists do, in fact, hire law students for the summer. The book tells you nothing about the work of an agency. And in most cases it will direct you to a personnel office or a summer coordinator responsible for receiving applications from all students, not just law students.

If you are interested in finding a summer job with a federal agency, read, or reread, Chapter 6 on Government, including the resource listings.

Appendix: Resources

Martindale-Hubbell Law Directory, Martindale-Hubbell, Inc., Summit, N.J. 07901 (Annual).

Directory of San Francisco Lawyers, The Bar Association of San Francisco, 220 Bush Street, San Francisco, Ca. 94104 (Annual).

The Association of the Bar of the City of New York — Year Book, 42 West 44th Street, New York, N.Y. 10036 (Annual).

American Bar Association Directory, ABA, 1155 East 60th Street, Chicago, Ill. 60637 (Annual) (The information contained in the *Directory* can also be found in Volume VI of *Martindale-Hubbell*).

Directory of Opportunities in International Law, John Bassett Moore Society of International Law, University of Virginia School of Law, Charlottesville, Va. 22901 (Revised every couple of years).

Who's Who in Labor, Arno Press, 330 Madison Avenue, New York, N.Y. 10017 (1976).

Women's Organizations & Leaders Directory, Today Publications and News Service, Inc., National Press Building, Washington, D.C. 20045 (Biennial).

Guide to American Directories, B. Klein Publications, Inc., Box 8503, Coral Springs, Fla. 33065 (Triennial).

Publications of the American Blind Lawyers Association, 749 South Street, Roslindale, Mass. 02131 (Available in large print and on cassettes).

Encyclopedia of Associations, Gale Research Co., Book Tower, Detroit, Mich. 48226 (Annual).

National Trade and Professional Associations of the U.S. & Canada and Labor Unions, Columbia Books, Inc., 734 Fifteenth Street, N.W., Washington, D.C. 20005 (Annual).

Washington IV, Potomac Books, Inc., P.O. Box 40604, Washington, D.C. 20016 (1975 — updated every few years).

New Jersey Institute for Continuing Legal Education, 18 Washington Place, Newark, N.J. 07102.

California Continuing Education of the Bar, 2150 Shattuck Avenue, Berkeley, Ca. 94705.

Practising Law Institute, 810 Seventh Avenue, New York, N.Y. 10019.

American Law Institute, 4025 Chestnut Street, Philadelphia, Pa. 19104.

New York Law Journal, New York Law Publishing Company, 233 Broadway, New York, N.Y. 10007 (Daily).

Los Angeles Daily Journal, 210 S. Spring Street, Los Angeles, Ca. 90012 (Daily).

The Arbitration Journal, The American Arbitration Association, Inc., 140 West 51st Street, New York, N.Y. 10020 (Quarterly).

The Journal of Taxation, 125 East 56th Street, New York, N.Y. 10022 (Monthly).

National Journal of Criminal Defense, National College of Criminal Defense Lawyers and Public Defenders, College of Law, University of Houston, Houston, Texas 77004 (Semi-annual).

Securities Regulation Law Journal, Warren, Gorham & Lamont, 210 South Street, Boston, Mass. 02111 (Quarterly).

Anti-Trust Law Journal, Section of Anti-Trust Law,

ABA, 1155 East 60th Street, Chicago, Ill. 60637 (Three times a year).

The Bulletin, The Copyright Society of the U.S.A., Law Center of New York University, 40 Washington Square South, New York, N.Y. 10011 (Bimonthly).

Juris Doctor, MBA Communications, Inc., 730 Third Avenue, New York, N.Y. 10017 (Monthly).

American Bar Association Journal, 77 South Wacker Drive, Chicago, Ill. 60606 (Monthly).

Case & Comment, The Lawyers Co-operative Publishing Company/Bancroft-Whitney Company, Rochester, N.Y. 14603 (Bimonthly).

Outside Counsel: Inside Director, Law Journal Press, 233 Broadway, New York, N.Y. 10007 (1974).

Practicing Law in New York City, The Council of New York Law Associates, 36 West 44th Street, New York, N.Y. 10036 (1975).

How To Go Directly Into Solo Practice Without Missing a Meal, Gerald M. Singer, Lawyers Co-operative Publishing Company/Bancroft-Whitney Company, Rochester, N.Y. 14603 (1976).

How To Start and Build a Law Practice, Jay G. Foonberg, 8530 Wishire Boulevard, Beverly Hills, Ca. 90211 (1976).

I'd Rather Do It Myself: How to Set Up Your Own Law Firm, Stephen Gillers, Law Journal Press, 233 Broadway, New York, N.Y. 10007 (1977).

Federal Career Directory, U.S. Civil Service Commission, Washington, D.C. 20415.

Federal Government Legal Career Opportunities, Law Student Division, American Bar Association, 1155 East 60th Street, Chicago, Ill. 60637 (Annual).

United States Government Manual, Superintendent of Documents, U.S. Government Printing Office, Washington, D.C. 20402 (Annual).

GOVERNMENT

Federal

Telephone directories of federal agencies, available from Superintendent of Documents, U.S. Government Printing Office, Washington, D.C. 20402 (Quarterly).

Congressional Directory, Superintendent of Documents, U.S. Government Printing Office, Washington, D.C. 20402 (Annual).

United States Lawyers Reference Directory, Legal Directories Publishing Company, Inc., 1314 Westwood Boulevard, Los Angeles, Ca. 90024 (Annual).

Martindale-Hubbell, see resources for Chapter 5.

Who's Who in Government, Marquis Who's Who, Inc., 200 East Ohio Street, Chicago, Ill. 60611 (1975 — new edition published every few years).

Congressional Staff Directory, P.O. Box 62, Mount Vernon, Virginia 22121 (Annual — *Advance Locator* offered each year as a pre-publication supplement).

The National Directory of Law Enforcement Administrators, The National Police Chiefs and Sheriffs Information Bureau, Association of Commerce Building, 828 N. Broadway, Milwaukee, Wis. 53202 (Annual).

Register — Department of Justice and the Courts of the United States, Superintendent of Documents, U.S. Government Printing Office, Washington, D.C. 20402 (Annual).

Publications of various federal agencies, available directly from each agency.

Placement Service Newsletter, Federal Bar Association, Placement Service, 1815 H Street, N.W., Washington, D.C. 20006 (Monthly).

State and Local State blue books, available from the Secretary of State of each state.

State Blue Books and Reference Publications (A

Selected Bibliography), The Council of State Governments, P.O. Box 11910, Iron Works Pike, Lexington, Kentucky 40511 (1974).

The City of New York Official Directory, The City Record, Office of Communications Service, Municipal Building, New York, N.Y. 10007 (Revised periodically).

Guide to American Directories, see resources for Chapter 5.

The National Directory of State Agencies, Information Resources Press, 2100 M Street, N.W., Washington, D.C. 20037 (Biennial).

Who's Who in Government, see resources under "Federal Government" for Chapter 6.

The National Directory of Law Enforcement Administrators, see resources under "Federal Government" for Chapter 6.

The National Directory of Prosecuting Attorneys, The National District Attorneys Association, 211 East Chicago Avenue, Chicago, Ill. 60611 (Annual).

Selected Statistics on the Office of Attorney General, National Association of Attorneys General, Committee on the Office of Attorney General, 3901 Barrett Drive, Raleigh, N.C. 27609 (1975).

Martindale-Hubbell, see resources for Chapter 5.

PUBLIC INTEREST

General

Information Resources for Public Interest, Commission for the Advancement of Public Interest Organizations, 1875 Connecticut Avenue, N.W., Washington, D.C. 20009 (Updated periodically).

Human Rights Organizations & Periodicals Directory, Meiklejohn Civil Liberties Institute, Box 673, Berkeley, Ca. 94701 (Biennial).

Encyclopedia of Associations, see resources for Chapter 5.

Harvard Law School Public Interest Questionnaire,

Placement Office, Harvard Law School, Cambridge, Mass. 02138 (Annual).

Law Students Civil Rights Research Council Report, LSCRRC, 52 Fairlie Street, Rm. 350, Atlanta, Ga. 30303 (Annual).

Alternatives, American Bar Association Consortium on Legal Services and the Public, 1155 East 60th Street, Chicago, Ill. 60637 (Bimonthly).

Legal Services Programs

Clearinghouse Review, National Clearinghouse for Legal Services, 500 North Michigan Avenue, Chicago, Ill. 60611 (Monthly).

Nlada Briefcase and *Nlada Washington Memo*, National Legal Aid and Defender Association, 2100 M Street, N.W., Washington, D.C. 20037 and 1155 East 60th Street, Chicago, Ill. 60637 (Monthly and bimonthly, respectively).

Directory of Legal Aid and Defender Offices, National Legal Aid and Defender Association, 2100 M Street, N.W., Washington, D.C. 20037 and 1155 East 60th Street, Chicago, Ill. 60637 (Updated periodically, and also reproduced in Volume VI of *Martindale-Hubbell*).

Legal Services Corporation Program Directory, Legal Services Corporation, 733 Fifteenth Street, N.W., Washington, D.C. 20005 (Updated periodically).

ACTION Domestic Programs Fact Book, Office of Domestic & Anti-poverty Operations, ACTION, 806 Connecticut Avenue, N.W., Washington, D.C. 20525 (Semi-annual).

Legal Services Corporation News, 733 Fifteenth Street, N.W., Washington, D.C. 20005 (Published periodically).

The Law & The Poor, Community Action for Legal Services, Inc., 335 Broadway, New York, N.Y. 10013 (Published periodically).

Publications of the National Legal Aid and Defender Association, see resources under "Legal Services Programs" for Chapter 7.

Poverty Law Reporter, Commerce Clearing House, 4025 W. Peterson Avenue, Chicago, Ill. 60646 (Updated periodically).

State and Locally Funded Legal Aid

Balancing the Scales of Justice: Financing Public Interest Law in America, The Council for Public Interest Law, 1250 Connecticut Avenue, N.W., Washington, D.C. 20036 (1976).

Public Interest Law: Five Years Later, American Bar Association Special Committee on Public Interest Practice and The Ford Foundation, Ford Foundation, 320 East 43rd Street, New York, N.Y. 10017 (1976).

"Lawyers for Social Change: Perspectives on Public Interest Law," Robert L. Rabin, 28 *Stanford Law Review* 207 (1976).

Martindale-Hubbell, Volume VI, "Public Interest Practice Firms and Organizations," see resources for Chapter 5.

Jobs in Social Change, Social and Educational Research Foundation, 3416 Sansom Street, Philadelphia, Pa. 19104 (1975).

The Foundation Grants Index, The Foundation Center, 888 Seventh Avenue, New York, N.Y. 10019 (Bimonthly — at the end of the year it is available in a bound, annual edition).

Conservation Directory, National Wildlife Federation, 1412 Sixteenth Street, N.W., Washington, D.C. 20036 (Annual).

Directory of Environmental Groups, U.S. Environmental Protection Agency, available from each regional office.

Pipeline, Council for Public Interest Law, 1250 Con-

Foundation Supported Public Interest Law Firms

necticut Avenue, N.W., Washington, D.C. 20036 (Quarterly).

Health Law Newsletter, National Health Law Program, 10995 Le Conte Avenue, Los Angeles, Ca. 90024 (Monthly).

Publications of the various Nader programs supported by Public Citizen, available from Public Citizen, Dupont Circle Building, Washington, D.C. 20036.

Annual Report, Center for Law and Health Sciences of Boston University School of Law, 209 Bay State Road, Boston, Mass. 02215 (Annual).

Docket of Cases, Natural Resources Defense Council, 15 W. 44th Street, New York, N.Y. 10036 (Annual).

Ecology Law Quarterly, School of Law, University of California, Berkeley, Ca. 94720 (Quarterly).

Columbia Journal of Environmental Law, Columbia University School of Law, 435 West 116th Street, New York, N.Y. 10027 (Semi-annual).

Columbia Journal of Law and Social Problems, Box 7, Columbia University School of Law, 435 West 116th Street, New York, N.Y. 10027 (Quarterly).

The Bulletin of the American Academy of Psychiatry and the Law, University of Pittsburgh School of Law, Pittsburgh, Pa. 15260 (Quarterly).

American Indian Law Review, College of Law, University of Oklahoma, 300 Timberdell Road, Norman, Okla. 73069 (Semi-annual).

Civil Rights and Civil Liberties Centers

Human Rights Organizations & Periodicals Directory, see resources under "General" for Chapter 7.

Balancing the Scales of Justice: Financing Public Interest Law in America, see resources under "Foundation-Supported Public Interest Law Firms" for Chapter 7.

Foundation Grants Index, see resources under

"Foundation-Supported Public Interest Law Firms" for Chapter 7.

Civil Rights Directory, U.S. Commission on Civil Rights, Washington, D.C. 20425 (Updated periodically).

Committee Report, Lawyers' Committee for Civil Rights Under Law, 733 Fifteenth Street, N.W., Washington, D.C. 20005 (Quarterly).

The Civil Liberties Review, ACLU, 22 East 40th Street, New York, N.Y. 10016 (Bimonthly).

Columbia Human Rights Law Review, Box 54, Columbia University School of Law, 435 West 116th Street, New York, N.Y. 10027 (Semi-annual).

Harvard Civil Rights — Civil Liberties Review, Austin Hall, Harvard Law School, Cambridge, Mass. 02138 (Three times a year).

Group Legal Services Programs (and Labor Unions)

Publications of the National Consumer Center for Legal Services, 1302 Eighteenth Street, N.W., Washington, D.C. 20036 (Include *Group Legal Review* and *Early Experiences With Group Legal Services*).

Group Legal Services, Susan T. Mackenzie, New York State School of Industrial and Labor Relations, Cornell University, Ithaca, N.Y. 14853 (1975).

Directory of National Unions and Employee Associations, U.S. Department of Labor, Bureau of Labor Statistics, 441 G Street, N.W., Washington, D.C. 20212 (Updated with supplements periodically).

National Trade and Professional Associations of the U.S. & Canada and Labor Unions, see resources for Chapter 5.

A Directory of Public Employee Organizations, U.S. Department of Labor, Labor Management Services Administration, Division of Public Employee

Labor Relations, 200 Constitution Avenue, N.W., Washington, D.C. 20216 (1974).

The Commonwealth of Massachusetts Directory of Labor Organizations, Massachusetts Department of Labor & Industry, State Office Building, 100 Cambridge Street, Boston, Mass. 02202 (Annual).

Directory of Employee Organizations in New York State, New York State Department of Labor, Division of Research and Statistics, 2 World Trade Center, New York, N.Y. 10047 (New edition published every few years).

Trade Union Handbook, New York City Central Labor Council AFL-CIO, 386 Park Avenue South, New York, N.Y. 10016 (Updated periodically).

Attorneys in Private Practice

Publications of the National Lawyers Guild, 853 Broadway, New York, N.Y. 10003 (Including *Guild Notes, Blind Justice, Guild Practitioner* and *Lawyers Referral Directory*).

Newsletter, The Council of New York Law Associates, 36 West 44th Street, New York, N.Y. 10036, Chicago Council of Lawyers, Monadnock Building, Suite 742, 53 W. Jackson Boulevard, Chicago, Ill. 60604 and Washington Council of Lawyers, 1000 Vermont Avenue, N.W., Washington, D.C. 20005.

Art & the Law, Volunteer Lawyers for the Arts, 36 West 44th Street, New York, N.Y. 10036 (Eight times a year).

CORPORATIONS

Law Practice in a Corporate Law Department, Committee on Corporate Law Departments, Corporation, Banking and Business Law Section, American Bar Association, 1155 East 60th Street, Chicago, Ill. 60637 (1971).

The Corporate Counsel Roster, The Law List Publishing Company, 740 South Fulton Avenue, Mt. Vernon, N.Y. 10550 (1972).

Martindale-Hubbell, see resources for Chapter 5.

The Fortune Double 500 Directory, Fortune Directories, Time-Life Building, Rockefeller Center, New York, N.Y. 10020 (Annual).

College Placement Annual, The College Placement Council, Inc., P.O. Box 2263, Bethlehem, Pa. 18001 (Annual).

Moody's Industrial Manual, Moody's Investors Service, Inc., 99 Church Street, New York, N.Y. 10007 (Annual).

Standard & Poor's Register of Corporations, Directors & Executives, Standard & Poor's Corporation, 345 Hudson Street, New York, N.Y. 10014 (Annual).

Classified Directory of Wisconsin Manufacturers, Manufacturers & Commerce, 111 East Wisconsin Avenue, Milwaukee, Wis. 53202 (Annual).

Industrial Directory of Virginia, Virginia State Chamber of Commerce, 611 East Franklin Street, Richmond, Va. 23219 (Biennial).

Directory of New England Manufacturers, George D. Hall Co., 20 Kilby Street, Boston, Mass. 02109 (Annual).

Chicago, Cook County and Illinois Industrial Directory, National Publishing Corp., 2720 Des Plaines Avenue, Des Plaines, Ill. 60018 (Annual).

Southern California Business Directory and Buyers Guide, Civic-Data Corp., P.O. Box 54045, Los Angeles, Ca. 90054 (Annual).

Moody's Bank & Finance Manual, Moody's Investors Service, Inc., 99 Church Street, New York, N.Y. 10007 (Annual).

Rand McNally International Bankers Directory, Rand McNally & Co., P.O. Box 7600, Chicago, Ill. 60680 (1976).

Polk's World Bank Directory, North American Edition, R.L. Polk & Co., 2001 Elm Hill Pike, P.O. Box 1340, Nashville, Tenn. 37202 (Semi-annual).

Directory of Trust Institutions, Trusts & Estates, 461 Eighth Avenue, New York, N.Y. 10001 (Annual).

Directory of American Firms Operating in Foreign Countries and *Directory of Foreign Firms Operating in the United States*, Simon & Schuster, Inc., 1230 Avenue of the Americas, New York, N.Y. 10020 (1975 and 1971 respectively).

The Business Lawyer, Section of Corporation, Banking and Business Law, American Bar Association, 1155 East 60th Street, Chicago, Ill. 60637 (Five times a year).

Encyclopedia of Associations, see resources for Chapter 5.

National Trade and Professional Associations of the U.S. & Canada, see resources for Chapter 5.

Journal of the Patent Office Society, P.O. Box 2600, Arlington, Va. 22202 (Monthly).

College Law Digest and *Journal of College Law*, National Association of College and University Attorneys, Suite 510, One Dupont Circle, N.W., Washington, D.C. 20036 (Bimonthly and quarterly respectively).

The Wall Street Journal, P.O. Box 300, Princeton, N.J. 08540 (Daily).

JUDICIAL CLERKSHIPS

The United States Law Week, The Bureau of National Affairs, Inc., 1231 Twenty-Fifth Street, N.W., Washington, D.C. 20037 (Weekly).

"Judicial Clerkships: A Symposium on the Institution," 26 *Vanderbilt Law Review* (Nov. 1973).

United States Court Directory, Administrative Office of the United States Courts, Supreme Court Building, Washington, D.C. 20544 (Annual).

Register — Department of Justice and Courts of the United States, see resources for Chapter 6.

United States Lawyers Reference Directory, see resources for Chapter 6.

Directory of State and Local Judges, National College of the State Judiciary, Judicial College Building, University of Nevada, Reno, Nevada 89507 (Annual).

Biographical Dictionary of the Federal Judiciary, Gale Research Co., Book Tower, Detroit, Mich. 48226 (1976).

Second Circuit Redbook, Federal Bar Council, 400 Park Avenue, New York, N.Y. 10022 (1975).

Congressional Directory, see resources for Chapter 6.

Who's Who in Government, see resources for Chapter 6.

California Courts and Judges, Law Book Service Co., 1001 Franklin Street, P.O. Box 14218, San Francisco, Ca. 94114 (Supplemented periodically).

State blue books, see resources for Chapter 6.

GRADUATE LAW AND FELLOWSHIP PROGRAMS

Graduate Law Study: Directory of Graduate Law Programs Offered Throughout the World, Prof. Michael Gordon, College of Law, University of Florida, Gainesville, Fla. 32601 (Updated periodically).

Survey and Directory of Clinical Legal Education 1975-1976, Council on Legal Education for Professional Responsibility, Inc., 280 Park Avenue, New York, N.Y. 10017 (1976).

ALTERNATIVE CAREERS

Administration

Martindale-Hubbell, see resources for Chapter 5.

The Wall Street Journal, see resources for Chapter 8.

Industrial directories, see resources for Chapter 8.

The New York Times, Section 4, "Careers in Education" (Sundays).

The Chronicle of Higher Education, 1717 Massachusetts Avenue, N.W., Washington, D.C. 20036 (Weekly).

The Spokeswoman, 53 West Jackson Boulevard, Suite 525, Chicago, Ill. 60604 (Monthly).

The Foundation Directory, The Foundation Center, 888 Seventh Avenue, New York, N.Y. 10019 (Biennial).

Foundation Grants Index, see resources for Chapter 7 under "Foundation-Supported Public Interest Law Firms."

Directory of National Unions and Employee Associations, see resources for Chapter 7 under "Group Legal Services Programs (and labor unions)."

Encyclopedia of Associations, see resources for Chapter 5.

Information Resources for Public Interest, see resources for Chapter 7 under "General."

Teaching

The New York Times (Sunday), *The Chronicle of Higher Education* and *The Spokeswoman*, all listed above under "Administration."

Placement Bulletin, Association of American Law Schools, Suite 370, One Dupont Circle, Washington, D.C. 20036 (Bimonthly).

Survey and Directory of Clinical Legal Education 1975 — 1976, see resources for Chapter 10.

Law Enforcement and Criminal Justice Education Directory, International Association of Chiefs of Police, Inc., 11 Firstfield Road, Gaithersburg, Md. 20760 (1975).

Research

Foundation Grants Index, see resources for Chapter 7 under "Foundation-Supported Public Interest Law Firms."

Annual Report, National Center for State Courts, 1660 Lincoln Street, Denver, Colo. 80264 (Annual).

Consultants and Consulting Organizations Directory, **Consulting**
Gale Research Co., Book Tower, Detroit, Mich.
48226 (1976).

Directory of Registered Federal and State Lobbyists, **Lobbying**
Marquis Academic Media, 4300 West 62nd Street,
Indianapolis, Ind. 46268 (1973).

College Placement Annual, see resources for Chap. 8. **Accounting**

"Lawbook Publishing: A $145 Million-a-Year Busi- **Publishing**
ness," Richard Sandza, *Juris Doctor,* Feb. 1974,
MBA Communications, Inc., 730 Third Avenue,
New York, N.Y. 10017.

The New York Times, Section 4, "Librarian Open- **Law**
ings" (Sunday). **Librarianship**
Directory of Law Libraries, American Association of
Law Libraries, 53 West Jackson Boulevard,
Chicago, Ill. 60604 (Biennial).
*Directory of Special Libraries and Information Cen-
ters,* Gale Research Company, Book Tower, De-
troit, Mich. 48226 (Supplemented periodically).

Harvard Law School Public Interest Questionnaire, **SUMMER AND**
see resources for Chapter 7 under "General." **PART-TIME**
Summer Jobs — Opportunities in the Federal Gov- **JOBS**
ernment, U.S. Civil Service Commission, Washington, D.C. 20415 (Annual).